ENGLISH in Common

Workbook

Mark Foley and Diane Hall

Series Consultants
María Victoria Saumell and Sarah Louisa Birchley

ALWAYS LEARNING   PEARSON

English in Common 2
Workbook

Pearson Education, 10 Bank Street, White Plains, NY 10606

Staff credits: The editorial, design, production, and manufacturing people who make up the *English in Common 2* team are Margaret Antonini, Allen Ascher, Rhea Banker, Eleanor Kirby Barnes, Mike Boyle, Tracey Cataldo, Aerin Csigay, Mindy DePalma, Dave Dickey, Chris Edmonds, Mike Kemper, Laurie Neaman, Loretta Steeves, Leigh Stolle, and Charlie Green.

This series is dedicated to Charlie Green. Without Charlie's knowledge of pedagogy, strong work ethic, sense of humor, patience, perseverance, and creativity, *English in Common* would never have existed.

Cover design: Tracey Cataldo
Cover photo: © qushe/shutterstock.com
Text design: Tracey Cataldo
Text composition: TSI Graphics
Text font: MetaPlus

ISBN 13: 978-0-13-262871-6
ISBN 10: 0-13-262871-6

Library of Congress Cataloging-in-Publication Data
Bygrave, Jonathan
    English in common. Book 1 / Jonathan Bygrave.
        p. cm.
    ISBN 0-13-247003-9—ISBN 0-13-262725-6—
ISBN 0-13-262727-2—ISBN 0-13-262728-0—
ISBN 0-13-262729-9—ISBN 0-13-262731-0
1. English language--Textbooks for foreign speakers.
2. English language--Grammar.
3. English language--Spoken English.
    PE1128.B865 2011
    428.24--dc23

2011024736

Printed in the United States of America
1 2 3 4 5 6 7 8 9 10—V001—16 15 14 13 12

Photo Credits: Page 4 (A) Shutterstock.com, (B) Shutterstock.com, (C) Shutterstock.com, (D) Press Association Images; p. 6 Tony Esparza/CBS/Photofest; p. 7 Michael Prince/Corbis; p. 9 Shutterstock.com; p. 10 (left) Shutterstock.com, (inset) Chabruken/Getty Images; p. 17 Shutterstock.com; p. 20 (all) Shutterstock.com; p. 21 ACI; p. 56 (all) Shutterstock.com; p. 59 Bruce Coleman/FLPA Images of Nature; p. 60 Shutterstock.com; p. 66 Pearson Education; p. 68 Courtesy J D Corporation; p. 70 BAA Aviation Photo Library; p. 74 Pearson Education; p. 77 Creatas/Alamy.

Illustration Credits: 90°, Enrique Krause, Álvaro Núñez, Juan Pardo, René Quirós, Pablo Torrecilla.

Contents

Vocabulary

1a Complete the country names. What is the letter in the center?   ?

A	U	S	T	R	A	L			A			
	C	O							A			
			M						C			
			S									
					V							M

b Complete the crossword with nationality words.

Across
5. Nicole Kidman
6. Will Smith
10. Gérard Depardieu
11. Gael García Bernal

Down
1. Paulo Coelho
2. Gong Li
3. ~~Hideki Matsui~~
4. Penélope Cruz
7. Andrea Bocelli
8. Helen Mirren
9. Ralf Schumacher

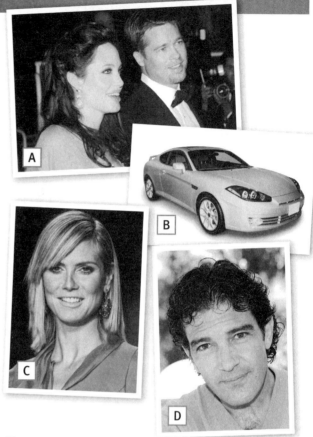

A

B

C

D

Grammar

2 Match the questions to the answers. Then match the answers to the photos.

  _D_ 1. Who is he?
  ____ 2. Who is she?
  ____ 3. What is it?
  ____ 4. Who are they?

  a. a sports car
  b. Antonio Banderas
  c. Brad Pitt and Angelina Jolie
  d. Heidi Klum

3 Complete the questions and answers with the words in the box.

Where	German	are	from	is
American	Spain	He's	She's	

1. Where _____ Brad Pitt and Angelina Jolie from? They're _____ the United States. They're _____.
2. Where _____ Antonio Banderas from? _____ from _____. He's Spanish.
3. _____ is Heidi Klum from? _____ from Germany. She is a _____ model.

Communication

4a Read the conversations. Complete the map below with the names in the box.

> **Map–Exercise 1**
> A: Hello. I'm Maria. I'm Mexican. I'm from Veracruz. What's your name?
> B: My name is Takumi. I'm from Tokyo. I'm Japanese.
> **Map–Exercises 2–3**
> A: Hi, I'm Claudio. I'm Italian. I'm from Rimini.
> B: Hi, Claudio. We're John and Liz.
> C: We're British. We're from London.
> **Map–Exercises 4–5**
> A: Hello, my name is Elda. I'm from São Paulo. I'm Brazilian. What's your name?
> B: I'm Jean Pierre. I'm from Montreal. I'm Canadian.

> ~~Maria~~   Takumi   John and Liz
> Elda   Claudio   Jean Pierre

b Correct the mistakes.

 1. I'm Maria. I'm ~~Portuguese~~. I'm from Veracruz. _Mexican_

 2. My name is Takumi. I'm from Tokyo. I'm Russian. _____

 3. I'm Claudio. I'm American. I'm from Rimini. _____

 4. We're John and Liz. We're British. We're from Manchester. _____

 5. My name is Elda. I'm from São Paulo. I'm Argentinian. _____

 6. I'm Jean Pierre. I'm from Montreal. I'm French. _____

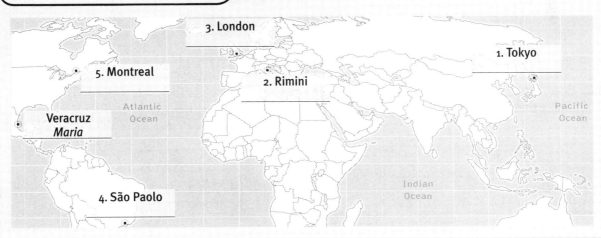

3. London

1. Tokyo

5. Montreal

2. Rimini

Atlantic Ocean

Pacific Ocean

Veracruz
Maria

Indian Ocean

4. São Paolo

Grammar

5 Complete the questions.

Ex: What _is it_____? It's a digital camera.

1. Where _____? He's from Mexico.
2. Where _____? They're from Korea.
3. What _____? It's a sports car.
4. Who _____? She's Jennifer Lopez.
5. What _____? They're students.
6. Where _____? I'm from Colombia.
7. What _____? He's a student.
8. What _____? They're photos.

6 Write the full forms.

Ex: she's _she is_____

1. we're _____
2. I'm _____
3. he's _____
4. they're _____
5. you're _____
6. it's _____

7 Correct the mistakes.

Ex: He's from Spain. He ~~am~~ Spanish. _is_____

1. I'm Gia. I'm of Italy. _____
2. We're students; we is Japanese. _____
3. Where be you from? _____
4. It am a cell phone. _____
5. Brad Pitt—who are he? _____

Vocabulary

Raymond

The Barone Family

Debra is Raymond's wife.

Robert is Raymond's brother.

Marie and Frank are Raymond
and Robert's parents.

Ally is Raymond and Debra's daughter.

Geoffrey and Michael are
Raymond and Debra's sons.

Robert is Ally's uncle.

Grammar

1a Read about the Barone family and complete the family tree.

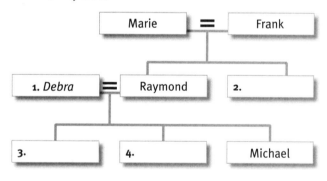

| Marie | **=** | Frank |

| 1. *Debra* | **=** | Raymond | 2. |

| 3. | 4. | Michael |

b Complete the sentences.

Ex: Ally is Michael's ___*sister*___ .

1. Michael is _____ brother.
2. Debra is _____ sister-in-law.
3. Raymond is Debra's _____ .
4. Ally is Robert's _____ .
5. Ally, Geoffrey, and Michael are Debra's

_____ .

6. Michael is Robert's _____ .
7. Marie is _____ mother-in-law.
8. _____ is Debra's father-in-law.
9. _____ is Ally's father.
10. Robert is Frank and Marie's _____ .

2a Complete the chart with family words.

Family word	Father's or mother's . . .
aunt	1. *sister*
uncle	2.
grandfather	3.
grandmother	4.

b Write sentences using the cues.

Ex: Jack/Hilary/husband
 Jack is Hilary's husband.

1. Stefan/Ana/brother

_____

2. Giorgio and Sophia/Mario/parents

_____

3. Louisa/Mr. and Mrs. Moreno/daughter

_____

4. Hana/Kwan/sister

_____

5. Alejandro and Elena/Manu/children

_____

6. Jorge and Miguel/Claudia/sons

_____

7. Stephanie/Pierre/niece

_____

3a Look at the picture. Match the conversations to the things in the picture.

Ex: __B__ Is this your car? — Yes, it's our car.

_____ 1. Is this your car? — No, it's his car.

_____ 2. Is this your house? — Yes, it's our house.

_____ 3. Is this your house? — No, it's her house.

b Circle the correct underlined word.

Ex: A is *my*/*their* house.

1. B is *her*/*their* car.
2. C is *her*/*his* car.
3. D is *her*/*his* house.

4 Correct the underlined mistakes. Use possessive adjectives.

Ex: Is you sister married? __your__

1. Are he brothers and sisters Canadian?

_____

2. Is she house in New York? _____

3. This is I dictionary. _____

4. Jennifer is we cousin. _____

5. Is this you cell phone? _____

5 Match the questions to the answers.

__d__ 1. Is Elizabeth your sister?

_____ 2. Are Sally and John your parents?

_____ 3. Is David your brother?

_____ 4. Are you a student?

_____ 5. Are we in the same class?

_____ 6. Are Elizabeth and Marie your cousins?

a. Yes, I am.

b. Yes, we are.

c. No, they're my sisters.

d. Yes, she is.

e. Yes, they are.

f. No, he's my boyfriend.

Communication

6 Read the email messsage. Then answer the questions.

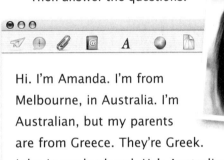

Hi. I'm Amanda. I'm from Melbourne, in Australia. I'm Australian, but my parents are from Greece. They're Greek. John is my husband. He's Australian, but his parents are from the United States. Our house is in Sydney. I'm a student at the University of Sydney.

Ex: Where is Amanda from?
She's from Melbourne.

1. Is Amanda Australian?

_____

2. Where are her parents from?

_____

3. What is her husband's name?

_____

4. Is he from the United States?

_____

5. Where are his parents from?

_____

6. Where is their house?

_____

7. Is Amanda a student?

_____

Vocabulary

1 Look at the pictures and the scrambled letters. Write the jobs.

1. T R E D I E R — *retired*
2. D R I X A T V E R I — _____
3. S U N E R — _____
4. S T I D E N T — _____

5. M R O P G E M A R R — _____
6. R E O C L O I P E F I C F — _____
7. N I N G E R E E — _____
8. H E R C A T E — _____

Grammar

2 <u>Underline</u> the mistakes. Then correct them.

> **Ex:** My brother is <u>student</u>. *a student*
>
> Sam's <u>a</u> electrician. *an electrician*

1. My cousin Julia's an nurse. _____
2. My grandfather is a retired. _____
3. Pablo's engineer in Bogatá. _____
4. My father's a unemployed. _____
5. Lucia's friend is lawyer in New York. _____
6. I'm an clerk in my uncle's store. _____
7. Kim wants to be a architect. _____
8. Is that police officer? _____

3a Write true sentences using the chart.

	~~Gerhard Richter~~		Australian	writer
1.	Jorge Amado		American	baseball player
2.	Kylie Minogue	is a	Japanese	~~artist~~
3.	Johnny Depp	an	Brazilian	pop star
4.	Ichiro Suzuki		~~German~~	actor

> **Ex:** *Gerhard Richter is a German artist.*
>
> 1. _____
> 2. _____
> 3. _____
> 4. _____

b Write more sentences using the jobs in Exercise 3a or the jobs in the box.

> architect   doctor   police officer
> journalist   lawyer   teacher

1. _____
2. _____
3. _____
4. _____

4 Put the words in the correct order to make sentences. Use contracted forms.

> Ex: Eduardo/not/married/Angela/are/and
> *Eduardo and Angela aren't married.*

1. My/20 Cedar Drive/not/address/is

   _____

2. retired/grandparents/are/My/not

   _____

3. little/tall/is/sister/My/not

   _____

4. from/not/Colombia/is/Eva

   _____

5. doctor/not/is/My/nephew/a

   _____

6. Canadian/not/My/are/parents

   _____

Reading and Writing

5a Read about Steven and fill in the blanks with the words in the box.

> old   email   from   manager
> cell   ~~name~~   phone   married

Hello, my *name*

is steven nagano. I'm 24 years
_____ (1.), and I'm
_____ (2.) concord
in massachusetts. I was born
there. I'm the _____ (3.) of a little
bookstore. I have a degree in english from
Boston University. I'm not _____ (4.).
My home is with my parents at 11 walden
Road in concord. My _____ (5.)
address is s.nagano@mail.com. My home
_____ (6.) number is 617-555-4472
and my _____ (7.) phone number is
617-555-2284.

b In English, we use capital letters at the beginning of people and places. Find six more mistakes with capital letters in Steven's story.

> Ex: steven = Steven

1. _____   4. _____
2. _____   5. _____
3. _____   6. _____

6a Read Steven's story in Exercise 5a again and complete the website form for Steven.

Perfect Partners on the Net

1. First name: *Steven*
2. Last name:
3. Age:
4. Place of origin:
5. Nationality:
6. Married ☐ Single ☐
7. Address:
8. Email address:
9. Telephone number (home):
10. Telephone number (cell):
11. Occupation:

b Complete this form for yourself.

Perfect Partners on the Net

1. First name:
2. Last name:
3. Age:
4. Place of origin:
5. Nationality:
6. Married ☐ Single ☐
7. Address:
8. Email address:
9. Telephone number (home):
10. Telephone number (cell):
11. Occupation:

7 Write an email in response to Steven.

_____
_____
_____
_____
_____
_____
_____
_____

UNIT 2
Work and leisure

LESSON 1

Grammar

1a Daniel is 32. He is the manager of the resort hotel Club Sol. Read about his daily routine.

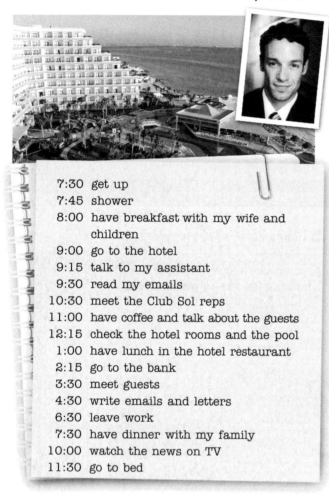

```
7:30   get up
7:45   shower
8:00   have breakfast with my wife and
       children
9:00   go to the hotel
9:15   talk to my assistant
9:30   read my emails
10:30  meet the Club Sol reps
11:00  have coffee and talk about the guests
12:15  check the hotel rooms and the pool
1:00   have lunch in the hotel restaurant
2:15   go to the bank
3:30   meet guests
4:30   write emails and letters
6:30   leave work
7:30   have dinner with my family
10:00  watch the news on TV
11:30  go to bed
```

You are Daniel. Answer the questions.

Ex: When do you get up?
I get up at seven thirty.

1. What do you do at a quarter to eight?

   _____

2. When do you go to work?

   _____

3. What do you do at a quarter past twelve?

   _____

4. Where do you have lunch?

   _____

5. What do you do after dinner?

   _____

b You are Daniel. Write short answers.

Ex: Do you have breakfast at eight thirty?
No, I don't.

1. Do you have breakfast in a hotel?

   _____

2. Are you a hotel manager?

   _____

3. Do you have a family?

   _____

4. Do you have lunch in a restaurant?

   _____

5. Do you leave work at six o'clock?

   _____

c Read the questions in Exercises 1a and 1b again. Write true answers about yourself on a separate piece of paper.

2 Match the questions to the answers.

_e_ 1. Are you single?   a. In an office.

___ 2. What do you do   b. At eight thirty.
        in the evening?
                               c. I have dinner with
___ 3. When do you go   my husband.
        to work?
                               d. I'm a computer
___ 4. Do you work in a   programmer.
        school?
                               e. No, I'm not.
___ 5. Where do you work?   f. No, I don't.

___ 6. What do you do?

3 Rewrite the sentences as questions. Then write a short affirmative (✓) or negative (✗) answer.

Ex: You get up at nine o'clock. (✓)
Do you get up at nine o'clock? Yes, I do.

We have a DVD player. (✗)
Do we have a DVD player? No, we don't.

1. You live in New York. (✗)

   _____

   _____

2. We have a Spanish dictionary. (✗)

   _____

   _____

3. You like all-inclusive vacations. (✓)

   _____

   _____

Communication

4a Read the interview with Daniel. Circle the *wh-* question words.

> **Lisa:** Daniel. Tell me about your routine.
>
> **Daniel:** OK. Well, I get up at about seven thirty. I shower at a quarter to eight, and then I have breakfast with the family.
>
> **Lisa:** When do you start work?
>
> **Daniel:** I start work at nine.
>
> **Lisa:** What do you do in the morning?
>
> **Daniel:** I talk to my assistant and then I read my emails.
>
> **Lisa:** Do you meet people?
>
> **Daniel:** Yes, I meet the Club Sol reps at about ten thirty. We have coffee at eleven o'clock in the office and talk about the guests. Then I check the hotel rooms and the swimming pool.
>
> **Lisa:** Do you eat in the hotel?
>
> **Daniel:** Yes, I do. In the hotel restaurant.
>
> **Lisa:** What do you do after lunch?
>
> **Daniel:** I go to the bank. Then I meet the hotel guests.
>
> **Lisa:** Do you work in the office?
>
> **Daniel:** Yes, I write emails and letters.
>
> **Lisa:** When do you go home?
>
> **Daniel:** I leave work at six thirty.
>
> **Lisa:** What do you do in the evening?
>
> **Daniel:** Well, I have dinner with my wife and children, and at ten o'clock I watch the news on TV.

b Check (✓) the questions or answers from the conversation.

Ex: __✓__ **a.** When do you start work?

_____ **b.** When you start work?

1. _____ **a.** What do you do in the morning?

   _____ **b.** What are you do in the morning?

2. _____ **a.** We have coffee at 11:00 in the hotel.

   _____ **b.** We have coffee at 11:00 in the office.

3. _____ **a.** I go to the bank. Then I meet the hotel guests.

   _____ **b.** I go to the bank and I meet the hotel guests.

4. _____ **a.** Do you work in office?

   _____ **b.** Do you work in the office?

5. _____ **a.** At 10:00 I watch the news on TV.

   _____ **b.** At 10:00 I watch movies on TV.

5 Write the questions for Daniel's answers.

Ex: _When do you start work?_

I start work at nine.

1. _____

   I talk to my assistant and read emails.

2. _____

   Yes, I meet the reps at ten thirty.

3. _____

   Yes, I eat in the hotel restaurant.

4. _____

   I leave work at six thirty.

5. _____

   I have dinner with my wife and children.

6. _____

   I watch the news at ten.

Vocabulary

6 Write questions and answers using the cues and the clocks.

Ex: you go bed? / I

When do you go to bed?

I go to bed at eleven thirty.

1. he get up? / He

   _____

   _____

2. she have lunch? / She

   _____

   _____

   _____

3. you leave the office? / I

   _____

   _____

   _____

4. we have dinner? / We

   _____

   _____

   _____

Vocabulary

1a Find more verbs in the word square and write them below. (→↓↘)

W	F	I	N	I	S	H	R
O	R	W	A	T	C	H	J
R	L	E	A	V	E	M	Q
K	G	O	A	S	V	A	W
M	E	E	T	D	H	K	F
B	T	S	L	F	E	E	D

Ex: _finish_

1. _____   6. _____
2. _____   7. _____
3. _____   8. _____
4. _____   9. _____
5. _____   10. _____

b Label the pictures with the words in the box and the verbs from Exercise 1a.

the children	~~hair~~	to bed
a newspaper	home	dinner

A

B

wash hair

C

D

E

F

Grammar

2a Complete the story with verbs from Exercise 1a.

Melanie has an interesting job—she's a hairdresser for movie stars, and she ___works___ in a movie studio. In the morning Melanie _____ (**1.**) up at seven o'clock. She _____ (**2.**) the children then has breakfast. She _____ (**3.**) home at eight thirty, and she gets to the movie studio at nine. Melanie _____ (**4.**) interesting people in her job. All day she _____ (**5.**) and dries the movie stars' hair. Sometimes in the afternoon she _____ (**6.**) movies in the studio. She _____ (**7.**) work at six o'clock, and she goes home. She _____ (**8.**) dinner, and in the evening she _____ (**9.**) the newspaper or listens to music—no movies for her! She _____ (**10.**) to bed at eleven thirty.

b Read about Melanie's day again and look at the pictures in Exercise 1b. Write the correct order of the pictures.

____ A ____ B ____ C ____ D _1_ E ____ F

Reading

3 Read about Julio's day. Then complete the chart.

I'm an assistant in a big electronics store. My day starts at six thirty—I <u>get up</u> and <u>shower</u>. Then I have breakfast at a quarter past seven, and I <u>leave</u> home at a quarter to eight. The store opens at eight thirty and I start work. I <u>work</u> in the home electronics part of the store, and I <u>sell</u> TVs, videos, and DVDs. I <u>like</u> my job—it's interesting, and I <u>talk</u> to a lot of people. I have lunch at twelve thirty, then I finish work at four thirty. I usually <u>play</u> basketball with friends for about an hour. I have dinner at six o'clock, and I <u>watch</u> TV in the evening. I <u>go</u> to bed at eleven o'clock.

Julio's day	
6:30	_Julio gets up and showers._
7:15	
7:45	
8:30	
12:30	
4:30	
6:00	
11:00	

Grammar

4a Put the words in the correct order to make questions.

> Ex: day/does/Julio's/start/What time/?
> *What time does Julio's day start?*

> he/7:oo/get up/Does/at/?
> *Does he get up at 7:oo?*

1. Where/Julio/does/work/?

2. the store/What time/open/does/?

3. sell/Does/cameras/he/?

4. Does/his job/he/like/?

5. after/he/does/work/do/What/?

6. he/do/What/at/does/6:oo/?

7. CDs/in the evening/Does/listen to/he/?

8. What/time/bed/he/does/go to/?

b Answer the questions in Exercise 4a.

> Ex: *Julio's day starts at six thirty.*
> *No, he doesn't. He gets up at six thirty.*

1.
2.
3.
4.
5.
6.
7.
8.

Writing

5 Sharon is an office assistant and a student. Use the information in the chart below to write about Sharon's day.

Morning—Office assistant for lawyer	
7:30	get up, have breakfast
8:30	walk to work
9:00	open the office
9:30–1:00	organize the lawyer's day, make phone calls
Afternoon—Spanish student	
2:00	go to Spanish class
5:00	leave school
6:30	have dinner
8:00–11:00	do homework, watch TV
11:15	go to bed

> Ex: *In the morning, Sharon is an assistant in a lawyer's office. She gets up at seven thirty and has . . .*

Vocabulary

1a Find and circle the words in the word chains.

1

bagreenewspaperedictionaryyellowalletelevision

2

usefulampicturescissorshoexcitingoldish

3

taxinterestingrayoungoodiscarefulaptop

b Complete the chart with the words from the word chains.

Objects	Color adjectives	Other adjectives
bag	green	

c What do these sentences describe? Use words from the Objects column.

Ex: It's a kind of computer. _laptop_

1. It's black and white, and we read it.

   _____

2. We look at these in museums. _____

3. We play it on a DVD player or a computer—it has music or movies on it. _____

4. This is yellow in New York. _____

5. We watch movies and sports on it.

   _____

6. We have this on the desk, to help us read.

   _____

7. You look up words in it. _____

Grammar

2a Match the questions to the pictures.

   _C_ 1. What's this?

   _____ 2. What's that?

   _____ 3. What are these?

   _____ 4. What are those?

A

B

C

D

b Use the pictures to answer the questions.

Ex: What's this? It's a . . .

   It's a book.

1. What's that?

   _____

2. What are these? They're . . .

   _____

3. What are those?

   _____

3 Complete the dialog with questions from Exercise 2b.

Woman: Hello. You have some nice things.
_____What's that_____? On the table?

Man: It's a printer. It's very good.

Woman: Oh, I think my niece wants a printer.
And _____ (1.)?

Man: They're discs, computer discs.

Woman: Very useful . . . and _____ (2.)?

Man: Oh, they're dishes.

Woman: Dishes?

Man: Yes, breakfast dishes.

Woman: But they're pink!

Man: Is that a problem?

Woman: No, no . . . _____ (3.)?

Man: It's a picture.

Woman: I know it's a picture, but what's the green thing?

Man: That's my old car. It's beautiful!

Woman: Hmm.

4a Complete the chart with plural forms. Use a dictionary to check.

	Singlular	Plural
1.	address	_addresses_
2.	car	
3.	city	
4.	family	
5.	foot	
6.	half	
7.	mouse	
8.	wife	
9.	scarf	
10.	sheep	
11.	suitcase	
12.	tomato	

b Complete the sentences. Make the nouns plural and change the verbs if necessary.

Ex: I always take one suitcase on vacation.
We always _take_ two
suitcases on vacation.

1. She has a problem with her foot.
They _____ problems with their
_____.

2. He wants to wash the car.
They _____ to wash the _____.

3. I like my red and green scarf.
We _____ our red and green
_____.

4. The vacation home is for one family.
The vacation homes _____ for two
_____.

5. Write your address on the form.
Write your _____ on the forms.

6. He always eats a tomato for lunch.
They always _____ _____ for
lunch.

Grammar

1 Look at the chart. Use it to complete the article with the positive or negative form of *like* or *go*.

Like				Go			
restaurants	cafés	nightclubs	sports centers	to concerts	shopping	for walks	to the gym
Andy ✓	✓	✗	✗	✓	✓	✗	✗
Rosa ✗	✓	✓	✓	✓	✗	✓	✓

I t's interesting that very different people sometimes meet and become friends . . . or husband and wife. Andy and Rosa are married, but they are very, very different.

Andy is a journalist, and he works a lot. In the evening he likes to relax. He doesn't want to be active. He _likes_____ restaurants and cafés, but he _doesn't like_____ nightclubs or sports centers. He doesn't dance or play sports. On the weekend he _____ (1.) to concerts, and he _____ (2.) shopping, but he _____ (3.) for walks or to the gym.

Rosa works in an office. Her job is very boring, and she likes to do exciting things in the evening and on weekends. In the evening she _____ (4.) to go to nightclubs or to the sports center, but she _____ (5.) restaurants. On the weekend, she _____ (6.) for walks and to the gym. Sometimes she _____ (7.) to a concert with Andy, but she _____ (8.) shopping at all.

2 Complete the story with the negative form of verbs in the box.

~~like~~	listen to	relax
speak	want to	watch

Evenings at home with all the family are awful! I like music, the radio, and the TV, but my daughter Sally _doesn't like____ the radio—she thinks it's boring. My mother _____ (1.) TV, and my children don't like that! My sister Helen _____ (2.) music. My husband and my father _____ (3.) talk to people in the evening, and my son Justin _____ (4.) to his sister because she doesn't like his friends. So, it's difficult for me in the evenings because I _____ (5.)!

3 Read about Isabel's activities and correct the sentences.

> I do lots of things on the weekend.
> I often meet my friends at the mall on Saturday morning, and we go shopping, then we have lunch at a café.
> Sometimes I play tennis in the park on Saturday afternoon, or I swim and sunbathe at the swimming pool.
> In the evening I go to a movie.
> On Sunday I like to relax, and I usually stay at home.

Ex: Isabel has lunch at home on Saturdays.
Isabel doesn't have lunch at home on
Saturdays. She has lunch in a café.

1. She plays tennis at the sports center.
   _____
   _____

2. She meets her friends at the gym.
   _____
   _____

3. She watches movies at home in the evening.
   _____
   _____

4. She swims at the beach.
   _____
   _____

5. She relaxes at a nightclub on Sundays.
   _____
   _____

Vocabulary

4a Complete the puzzle with days of the week. Which day isn't in the puzzle? Write it below.

Day not in the puzzle: _____

b Write the days of the week on the calendar pages.

Reading and Writing

5a Read about Kenji. Then complete his datebook.

My name's Kenji. I live in Japan. I'm very active. My week is very busy. On Mondays I go to the swimming pool. On Tuesdays I go to the gym, and then I go to a dance class. On Wednesdays I ride my bike in the mountains, but on Thursdays I stay at home and relax. On Fridays I play tennis or soccer with friends. On the weekend I usually go skiing.

Monday 4	Thursday 7
go to swimming pool	
Tuesday 5	**Friday 8**
Wednesday 6	**Saturday 9 / Sunday 10**

b Now look at Alana's datebook and write about her week. Use *and, but,* or *or.*

Monday 4	Thursday 7
watch TV/a DVD	go for a walk
Tuesday 5	**Friday 8**
listen to music and read a book	play video games with Carolina
Wednesday 6	**Saturday 9 / Sunday 10**
meet friends at a café	relax at home/ sunbathe on the beach

My name's Alana. I live in Brazil. I'm very relaxed. On Mondays, I _____
_____
_____
_____
_____
_____

Vocabulary

1a Look at the picture and match the activities to the nouns below.

_1_ **1.** karate   ____ **5.** yoga   ____ **8.** sailing

____ **2.** swimming   ____ **6.** dancing   ____ **9.** running

____ **3.** riding a bike   ____ **7.** soccer   ____ **10.** tennis

____ **4.** skateboarding

b Write the verbs for the activities, using *go, play,* or *do* if necessary.

A _go sailing_   E _____   H _____

B _____   F _____   I _____

C _____   G _____   J _____

D _____

2a Cross out the word that does not belong.

Ex: **do:** aerobics   karate   ~~sailing~~

1. go: swimming   riding my bike   running

2. play: dance   video games   tennis

3. do: soccer   yoga   aerobics

4. go: skiing   running   video games

5. play: soccer   tennis   yoga

b Correct the mistakes.

Ex: I ~~do sailing~~ every weekend. _go sailing_

1. We go riding our bikes to work.

_____

2. Do you play aerobics? _____

3. We swimming at the swimming pool.

_____

4. My brother does video games every evening. _____

5. They go karate twice a week. _____

Reading

3a Read the article then circle the correct title.

People say that members of a family often have the same abilities. Look at people in different jobs, and you can see that it's true. Here are some examples:

- In sports, we have the famous soccer brothers Gary and Phil Neville. In tennis, we have the Williams sisters, Venus and Serena. And in skiing, we have Maria and Susanne Riesch.

- In show business everyone knows Julia Roberts. Not everyone knows her brother Eric, but he also acts. Jaden Smith and his sister Willow are both actors and singers, and the brothers Joel and Ethan Coen are both famous for the interesting movies they make together.

- But it isn't only brothers and sisters— Kingsley Amis and his son Martin are both famous British writers, and Luke Russert, like his father, the late Tim Russert is a journalist in the US.

Famous Fathers and Sons   Famous Families
Famous Brothers and Sisters

b Match the people to the activities.

   _c_ **1.** Venus and Serena Williams   **a.** act.

                                b. sing and act.

      2. Julia and Eric Roberts   ~~**c.** play tennis.~~

      3. The Neville brothers   **d.** play soccer.

      4. Kingsley and Martin Amis   **e.** write books.

                                f. ski.

      5. The Coen brothers   **g.** make good movies.

      6. The Riesch sisters

      7. Jaden and Willow Smith

Grammar

4 Write sentences about the people in Exercise 3b, using *can*.

    Ex: *Venus and Serena Williams can both play tennis.*

    1. _____

    2. _____

3. _____

4. _____

5. _____

6. _____

5a Complete the dialog with *can* or *can't*.

A: Good morning, Miss Randall. Let me ask you a few questions. We have about 60 children here. ___*Can*___ you organize games for them?

B: Yes, I _____ (**1.**). I do that in my job now.

A: Great. How about your skills? Can you sing?

B: Yes, I _____ (**2.**) sing and dance. I can't paint, but I _____ (**3.**) draw.

A: OK. Now, sports. We want our organizers to help the children learn sports.

B: Well, I can ride a bike, and I _____ (**4.**) play tennis.

A: Good. Can you teach any other activities, for example, karate?

B: No, not karate, but I _____ (**5.**) teach aerobics.

A: Can you play the guitar?

B: No, I _____ (**6.**).

A: Now, we have children from other countries. Can you speak other languages?

B: Yes, I _____ (**7.**) speak German and Spanish.

A: French?

B: No, I _____ (**8.**) speak French.

A: OK. And can you drive?

B: Yes, I _____ (**9.**).

A: Thank you, Miss Randall. That's all for now.

b Which activities can and can't Miss Randall do? Make a list.

    Ex: *She can sing and dance.*

         She can draw, but she can't paint.

Communication

1a Read the phone conversations and messages. Then match them to the descriptions.

1

A: Thank you for calling your Tel-call voicemail service. You have one message.

B: Hi Daniel, it's Lucy. Can you call me this afternoon after twenty past two? My number's 940-555-8832. Thanks.

2

A: This is Phil and Isabel's phone. We're not here at the moment, so please leave a message with your name and number after the tone.

B: Phil? It's Lara. I can't see you tomorrow because there's an important meeting at my office. How about ten past seven on Friday? You can call me at 991-555-3445.

3

A: Hello. Davis and Davis.

B: Good afternoon. Can I speak to Michael Jenkins?

A: I'm afraid he's not here today. Can I take a message?

B: Yes. Can you ask him to call Dr. Gupta after four thirty?

A: Of course. What's your number?

B: It's 894-555-7701. Thanks.

A: Of course. Good-bye.

_____ a message on an answering machine

_____ a phone call to an office

_____ a voicemail message

b Read the phone calls again and complete the messages.

1
Caller: ____Lucy____
Phone number: _____
Message:
call her after 2:20 this afternoon

2
Caller: ____Lara____
Phone number: _____
Message:
She can't _____
How about _____

3
Caller: ___Dr. Gupta___
Phone number: _____
Message:

2 Find five more mistakes in this phone conversation and correct them.

A: Hello.

B: Hello. Can I speak ~~of~~ *to* Nam Park?

A: I'm afraid she isn't there today. Can I make a message?

B: Yes. Can you speak her to call Erik Langley at the bank?

A: Of course. What are your number?

B: I am 209-555-3301.

A: OK. Good-bye.

B: Bye.

Vocabulary

3a Match the numbers to the words.

_f_	**1.** 8,000	**a.**	eighty
_____	**2.** 800	**b.**	eighty thousand
_____	**3.** 80	**c.**	eight hundred thousand
_____	**4.** 800,000	**d.**	eight million
_____	**5.** 80,000	**e.**	eight hundred
_____	**6.** 8,000,000	**f.**	~~eight thousand~~

b Complete the sentences with the numbers in the box.

> 8,760   1,331,000,000   194,000,000
>
> 2001   ~~20,000,000~~   20,000

Ex: The population of Australia is _20,000,000_ .

1. My favorite film is Stanley Kubrick's

_____: A Space Odyssey.

2. _____ people live in Brazil.

3. Our favorite book is _____ Leagues under the Sea by Jules Verne.

4. A year has _____ hours.

5. _____ people live in China.

An epic drama of adventure and exploration

2001: a space odyssey
MGM PRESENTS A STANLEY KUBRICK PRODUCTION
CINERAMA Super Panavision® and Metrocolor

c Write out the numbers in Exercise 1b in words.

Ex: _twenty million_

1. _____

2. _____

3. _____

4. _____

5. _____

Writing

4 Write requests with the cues. Use *ask, come, meet,* or *take.*

Ex: to the office/tomorrow?

Can you come to the office tomorrow?

1. Anna/call me/after 6:30?

_____

_____

2. me/at the hospital/at 7:15?

_____

_____

3. Carla/call Mom and Dad/this weekend?

_____

_____

4. to the store/on Tuesday/after 5:00?

_____

_____

5. the children/to school/tomorrow?

_____

_____

5a Complete the sentences with the words in the box.

> don't   can   How   ~~we~~
> Let's   about   Why

_____ **Stephan:** No, I'm at work at 6:30. Why don't _we_ meet at eight o'clock?

_____ **Annabel:** OK. How _____ **(a.)** Luigi's Italian restaurant on Green Street?

_____ **Annabel:** _____ **(b.)** about dinner at the Chinese restaurant?

_1_ **Stephan:** What _____ **(c.)** we do tonight?

_____ **Stephan:** No, I don't like Chinese food. Why _____ **(d.)** we go to an Italian restaurant?

_____ **Annabel:** OK. _____ **(e.)** go to the Pizzeria on Nelson Street. Can you meet me at 6:30?

_____ **Annabel:** OK. Eight o'clock at the pizzeria.

_____ **Stephan:** No, I don't like Luigi's. _____ **(f.)** don't we go to a pizzeria?

b Number the sentences in the correct order.

Grammar

be: questions, answers, and negatives

1a Complete the sentences with *am, is, isn't, are,* or *aren't.*

_j_	1.	Where _is_ she from?	a.	No, he _____.
___	2.	How old _____ you?	b.	No, I _____ not.
___	3.	What _____ it?	c.	It _____ a cell phone.
___	4.	Who _____ he?	d.	Yes, she _____.
___	5.	_____ you married?	e.	He _____ Matt Damon.
___	6.	_____ she a student?	f.	No, they _____.
___	7.	_____ he Korean?	g.	They _____ cell phones.
___	8.	_____ they from Colombia?	h.	It _____ in Brazil.
___	9.	Where _____ São Paulo?	i.	I _____ 19.
___	10.	What _____ they?	j.	She _is_ ~~from Vietnam.~~

b Now match the questions to the answers.

Possessive *'s* and possessive adjectives

2 Circle the correct choice.

Ex: Is Michelle Obama Barack Obama's sister?
No, she's _her_/(his) wife.

1. Excuse me. Are you Maria's cousin?
No, I'm _her_/_his_ husband.
2. Is David _your_/_you_ son?
3. Is Elizabeth _their_/_their's_ grandmother?
4. Lily is _Antonio_/_Antonio's_ girlfriend.
5. I'm from England and _me_/_my_ wife is from Venezuela.
6. Gordon is a lawyer, but _his_/_their_ two sons are artists.
7. We are Canadian, but _my_/_our_ parents are from Korea.
8. Prince Harry is Prince _Williams_/_William's_ brother.
9. My sister and I live with _we_/_our_ grandfather.
10. Do you visit _your_/_you_ cousins in Peru?

Simple present

3 Complete the sentences with the correct form of the verb in parentheses.

Ex: Julia _watches_ television in the evening. (watch)
Stephen _doesn't like_ classical music. (not like)

1. My sister _____ in a restaurant. (work)
2. David _____ the bus to work. (not take)
3. We _____ at seven thirty. (get up)
4. I _____ dinner at eight o'clock. (have)
5. John _____ lunch in his office. (have)
6. Mrs. Dawson _____ to work by car. (go)
7. Sue _____ her car on Saturdays. (wash)
8. The children _____ to school on the weekend. (not go)
9. My mother _____ in the city. (not live)
10. I _____ traffic jams. (not like)

4 Write questions with the cues.

Ex: she/live/in London?
Does she live in London?

Where/he/eat lunch?
Where does he eat lunch?

1. William/leave home/at eight o'clock?

_____

2. Where/your parents/go on vacation?

_____

3. When/you/start work?

_____

4. you/work/in an office?

_____

5. she/have/a DVD player?

_____

6. What time/he/get home?

_____

7. When/Emily/eat dinner?

_____

8. Where/you/work?

_____

this/that/these/those

5 Look at the picture and complete the dialog with *this, that, these,* or *those.*

A: Do you like _these_____ lamps?

B: No, I like _____ lamp.

A: Do you like _____ chair?

B: No, I like _____ chairs.

Plural nouns

6 Write the plural forms in the correct columns.

	Add -s	Add -es	Change -f to -v and add -s or -es	Change -y to -i and add -es	Irregular
Ex: dress book	*books*	*dresses*			
1. child					
2. city					
3. party					
4. knife					
5. person					
6. picture					
7. scarf					
8. watch					

can/can't

7 Write questions and answers with the cues.

Ex: you/play tennis? (Yes)

Q: _Can you play tennis?_____

A: _Yes, I can._____

Hiroshi/speak French? (No)

Q: _Can Hiroshi speak French?_____

A: _No, he can't._____

1. you/sing? (Yes)

Q: _____

A: _____

2. your husband/cook? (No)

Q: _____

A: _____

3. you/do karate? (Yes)

Q: _____

A: _____

4. a DVD player/send emails? (No)

Q: _____

A: _____

Vocabulary

8a Check (✓) the correct box.

		Jobs	Family	Possessions	Verbs	Days
1.	accountant	✓	☐	☐	☐	☐
2.	daughters	☐	☐	☐	☐	☐
3.	do	☐	☐	☐	☐	☐
4.	finish	☐	☐	☐	☐	☐
5.	get up	☐	☐	☐	☐	☐
6.	teacher	☐	☐	☐	☐	☐
7.	play	☐	☐	☐	☐	☐
8.	Sunday	☐	☐	☐	☐	☐
9.	uncle	☐	☐	☐	☐	☐
10.	wallet	☐	☐	☐	☐	☐

b Complete the sentences with the words from Exercise 8a.

1. Caroline works in a school. She is a(n) _____ .

2. I'm a(n) _____; I work in an office.

3. My father's brother is my _____ .

4. We have two _____: Jane and Mary.

5. I have $50 in my _____ .

6. What time do you _____ in the morning?

7. We _____ work at six o'clock.

8. I _____ yoga at the gym.

9. We _____ tennis on Wednesdays.

10. Do you go to work on _____ ?

9 Match the activities to the places.

_____ 1. see a movie a. gym

_____ 2. dance b. concert hall

_____ 3. go for a walk c. theater

_____ 4. buy things d. beach

_____ 5. sunbathe e. restaurant

_____ 6. have dinner f. school

_____ 7. listen to music g. home

_____ 8. do aerobics h. park

_____ 9. watch TV i. store

_____ 10. learn English j. nightclub

Vocabulary

1 Find these things in the picture and write the words.

Ex: easy-to-prepare food
hot dog

1. fresh fruit _____
2. fish _____
3. vegetable _____
4. meat _____

2 Complete the food and drink words with letters in the box.

am	as	an	ea	ee	ee	el	il
ip	in	~~pp~~	tt	ff	od	gg	ic

Ex: a_pp_les

1. b____f
2. br____d
3. bu____er
4. ch____se
5. co____ee

6. s____a
7. ch____s
8. l____b
9. m____k
10. or____ge juice

11. p____ta
12. p____eapples
13. e____s
14. m____ons
15. r____e

Grammar

3 Complete the chart with the words from Exercise 2. One word can go in two places.

	Meat	Fruit	Drinks	Dairy	Other
Count		apples			
Noncount					

4 Correct the mistakes.

Ex: I drink a lot of ~~milks~~ every day. _milk_

1. Tea are popular in England. _____
2. We have a cereal for breakfast. _____
3. I buy a bag of rices every week. _____
4. Do you eat a lot of meats? _____
5. People say sugar are bad for you. _____
6. I need a loaf of breads. _____
7. I like a French bread. _____
8. Do you like tunas? _____
9. Are the bottled water cold? _____
10. Which melons is the best? _____

5 Complete the sentences with *How much* and *How many*.

Ex: _How much_ do you eat each day?

1. _____ bags of rice do you buy each month?
2. _____ bananas do you eat each week?
3. _____ mayonnaise do you like on your sandwich?
4. _____ pizzas do you order each month?
5. _____ cartons of milk do you drink each month?
6. _____ eggs do you eat each week?
7. _____ coffee do you drink in the morning?
8. _____ milk do you put on your cereal?

6 Write questions with *How much* or *How many*. Then write answers that are true for you.

Ex: apples/you/eat/every week

How many apples do you eat every week?
I eat three apples every week.

1. rice/you/buy/at the supermarket

_____?

_____

2. water/you/drink/each day

_____?

_____

3. oranges/you/buy/at the market

_____?

_____

4. bananas/your family/eat/each week

_____?

_____

5. coffee/you/drink/on the weekend

_____?

_____

6. eggs/you/buy/at the store

_____?

_____

7 This is Julia's weekly shopping list. Complete the questions and answers.

6 apples
2 bags rice
1 box of cereal
1 carton of milk
500g/1 lb coffee
3 bananas
12 eggs
4 oranges

Ex: How much milk does Julia buy?
She buys one carton.

1. _____?
She buys 500 grams/1 pound.

2. _____?
She buys four.

3. _____ does Julia buy?
_____ two bags.

4. _____ eggs _____?
_____.

5. _____ cereal _____?
_____.

6. _____?
_____ three.

7. _____?
_____ six.

Vocabulary

1a Unscramble the container words.

Ex: N A C   _can_

1. T O T L E B   _____
2. O X B   _____
3. C O R A N T   _____
4. A K G C A E P   _____
5. G A B   _____

b Label the pictures with words from Exercise 1a.

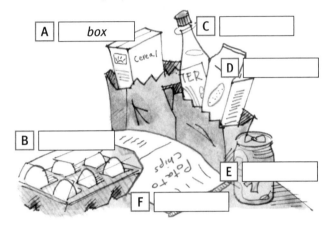

c Complete the phrases with container words.

1. a _____ of chips
2. a _____ of water
3. a _____ of eggs
4. a _____ of soda
5. a _____ of cookies
6. a _____ of cereal

Grammar

2 Look at the picture. Write the list of ingredients. Use *a/an* or *some* and the words in the box.

> butter   cheese   papaya   pasta   tuna
> salad   tomato   water   ~~pineapple~~

Ex: _a pineapple_

1. _____   5. _____
2. _____   6. _____
3. _____   7. _____
4. _____   8. _____

3 Complete the dialog with *a/an*, *some*, or *any* and the words in parentheses. Use the plural if necessary.

A: Let's write our shopping list for the supermarket.

B: OK. I think we want _some bottled water_ (bottled water).

A: No, we don't need _____ (**1.** bottled water). We have six bottles. We don't have _____ (**2.** fruit juice).

B: OK. Now, get some eggs and _____ (**3.** cheese)—we can have an omelette tonight.

A: Right. Do we have _____ (**4.** potatoes)?

B: Yes, we do. Oh, get _____ (**5.** chips) for my mother too—a nice big bag, please. Do you have _____ (**6.** money)?

A: Well, I don't have _____ (**7.** cash), but I have _____ (**8.** credit card).

B: OK. Do you want a cup of coffee before you go?

A: Yes, please! Can I have _____ (**9.** cookie), too—just one?

B: Sorry, we don't have _____ (**10.** cookies). Put cookies on the shopping list.

Reading

4 Read the letter from Jim, a magazine writer. Write short answers to the questions.

Dear Amanda,

I'm sorry to hear about your daughter, Jane. It's very bad that she goes out late all the time and doesn't come home until one in the morning, at the age of only 17. I can understand that she's tired every morning and doesn't want to go to school! Young people need a lot of sleep and your daughter doesn't get much. Also, a lot of fast food like burgers and pizza is not very healthy for a girl of her age. I think Jane is probably very unhappy. You need to talk to her and ask her some questions, for example, why does she hate school and why doesn't she do any homework? Why don't you take Jane out one evening to a nice restaurant and talk to her? She probably wants to talk to you but doesn't know how to begin.

Good luck,
Jim

Ex: Who is Jim's letter to?
   Amanda

1. Who is the letter about?
   _____

2. How old is Jane?
   _____

3. What does she do in the evenings?
   _____

4. How does she feel in the mornings?
   _____

5. What are the problems with her diet?
   _____

6. What does Jane think of school?
   _____

7. Does she do her homework?
   _____

Writing

5 Amanda's letter to the magazine describes her daughter and asks for Jim's help. Follow the steps to write her letter.

1. Complete the main part of the letter, about Jane's problems. (Use your answers to Exercise 4.)

2. Write the introduction and closing of the letter.

_____,

   I have a problem with my daughter, Jane. She's only _____,
but she hates _____
_____.
Also, she goes out _____
_____
_____
_____.
Her diet is also very bad. I give her healthy food at home, but she _____
_____
_____.
   What can I do? Please help me.

   _____

Communication

1a Read the phone conversation. Answer the questions.

Super Pizza:	Hello, Super Pizza.
Marisa:	Hi. How much is a large grilled chicken pizza?
Super Pizza:	That's eight ninety-five.
Marisa:	And how much is a small tomato salad?
Super Pizza:	Two forty-five.
Marisa:	What about coffee?
Super Pizza:	A small cup of coffee is two dollars, and a large coffee is two seventy-five.
Marisa:	OK. Do you have a pepper and onion pizza?
Super Pizza:	Yes.
Marisa:	How much is a large one?
Super Pizza:	Eight fifty.
Marisa:	Fine. I'd like a large pepper and onion pizza.
Super Pizza:	Any side orders?
Marisa:	Yes. Can I have a small salad?
Super Pizza:	Sure. What about a drink?
Marisa:	A small coffee, please.
Super Pizza:	Right. A large pepper and onion pizza, a small salad, and a small cup of coffee.
Marisa:	How much is that?
Super Pizza:	That's twelve ninety-five.
Marisa:	Can I pay by credit card?
Super Pizza:	Of course. What's the name on the card?
Marisa:	It's Marisa Sanchez . . .

1. Does Marisa order a pizza? _____
2. Does she order a drink? _____
3. How does Marisa pay for the food? _____

b Read the conversation again. What exactly does Marisa order? Complete the bill.

1 large _____ $_____
1 _____ salad $_____
1 _____ $ _2.00_
Total $_____

c Read the conversation again and complete the prices in the menu.

Super Pizza FREE DELIVERY!

cheese	$5.95	$6.95
spinach and mushroom	$6.75	$7.75
pepper and onion	$7.50	1. _____
grilled chicken	$7.95	2. _____
meatball	$8.25	$9.25

SIDE ORDERS
fries	$2.25	$3.35
salad	3. _____	$3.00
tuna salad	$3.00	$3.99

DRINKS
bottled water	$1.25	$2.15
coffee	4. _____	5. _____
soda	$1.95	$2.35

Call 970-555-0011 to order.
We accept all major credit cards or you can pay cash on delivery.

2a Write the questions for these answers. Use the information in the menu.

Ex: _How much is a small spinach and_
mushroom pizza?
It's $6.75.

1. _____
It's $8.50.

2. _____
It's $3.00.

3. _____
It's $8.25.

b Match the questions to the answers. Use the information in the menu.

_f_ 1. Do you have pizzas?
___ 2. Can I pay by credit card?
___ 3. How much is a large coffee?
___ 4. Do you have burgers?
___ 5. Anything to drink?
___ 6. Any side orders?

a. Yes, I'd like a bottled water.
b. No, we don't.
c. Yes, you can.
d. It's $2.75.
e. Yes, large fries, please.
f. ~~Yes, we do.~~

Grammar

3a You are Janine. This is the lunch order for your office. Read the notes and label the pictures with object pronouns.

Today's lunch order
• Janine: burger and fries
• Janine, Steve, and Lucy: 3 cups of coffee
• Peter: a cheeseburger
• Alicia: a tuna salad sandwich and a bottled water
• Linda and Erik: 2 small pizzas

for _me_

1. for _____   3. for _____

2. for _____   4. for _____

b You are Janine. Replace the word(s) in parentheses with object pronouns. Then write the answers.

Ex: Are the two small pizzas for (Lucy) _her_?
No, _they are for them_.

1. Are the fries for (Linda and Erik) _____?
No, _____.

2. Are the three cups of coffee for (Peter) _____?
No, _____.

3. Is the sandwich for (Janine, Steve, and Lucy) _____?
No, _____.

4. Is the cheeseburger for (Alicia) _____?
No, _____.

5. Is the bottled water for (Linda and Erik) _____?
No, _____.

4 Replace the underlined expressions with pronouns and rewrite the sentences.

Ex: Our grandmother and grandfather live with me and my brothers.
They live with us.

1. Daniel loves Ina.
_____

2. My boyfriend and I don't like meat.
_____

3. Our teachers help me and my classmates with our homework.
_____

4. My parents visit my grandparents every Saturday afternoon.
_____

5. My brothers and I play soccer with John.
_____

6. Mrs. Field uses her computer every day.
_____

7. Do you and your friends want to have lunch with me and my friends?
_____

5 Circle the correct choice.

A: Hello, what can I get you today?
B: I'd *want/like* (1.) a mushroom pizza, please.
A: Small or large?
B: How *much/many* (2.) is the large pizza?
A: It's $7.75.
B: OK, large, please.
A: Right. A large mushroom pizza. Any side orders?
B: *Are/Do* (3.) you have fries?
A: No, we don't. Do you *want/like* (4.) a salad?
B: OK. A small salad.
A: Anything to *eat/drink* (5.)?
B: Yes, *I'm/I'd* (6.) like a large cup of coffee, please.
A: OK.
B: How much *are/is* that (7.)?
A: That's $10.95.
B: Can I pay *by/of* (8.) credit card?

LESSON **1**

Reading

Las Palomas Village

Thank you for asking for information about Las Palomas Village.

Las Palomas is the perfect place for a vacation, or for a second home, especially for retired people. Only 17 miles from the airport, Las Palomas is perfect for long weekends, but it isn't just a resort—it's also a home.

At Las Palomas there's a small supermarket, and there's a bank. There are three cafés and two restaurants serving international food. There are two large swimming pools, and there's a well-equipped gym. You can also walk to the local beach in just five minutes, where you can find a variety of stores and restaurants. There isn't a movie theater or a hospital in the village, but these are only a short bus ride away.

There are 42 apartments at Las Palomas, with one, two, or three bedrooms, and there are four luxury villas. You can buy your apartment with furniture, if you want. The furniture includes all modern kitchen equipment, beds, sofas, dining tables, and chairs. Each apartment has a private balcony. Prices start from $200,000.

You can visit Las Palomas any time. Please call 986-555-4000 to schedule your visit.

1a Look at the information. Circle what it is.

an ad in a magazine   an answer to a letter

b Read about Las Palomas Village. What can you find there? Check (✓) the correct pictures.

1.   3.   5.   7.

2.   4.   6.   8.

c Read the letter again. Mark the sentences true (*T*) or false (*F*).

Ex: _F_ Las Palomas is in the city.

_____ 1. There aren't any stores at Las Palomas.

_____ 2. You can change money in the village.

_____ 3. You can walk to the beach.

_____ 4. There aren't any movie theaters.

_____ 5. You can't buy an apartment with furniture.

_____ 6. Each apartment has a private yard.

Vocabulary

2a Complete the furniture and home equipment words with the correct vowels (a, e, i, o, u) .

1. B __ T H T U B
2. B __ D
3. C D P L __ Y __ R
4. A R M C H __ __ __ R
5. S T __ V E
6. T __ B L __
7. DVD P L __ Y __ R
8. R E F R __ G __ R A T O R
9. M __ C R __ W __ V __
10. S __ F __
11. S H __ W __ R
12. B __ __ K S H __ L F

b Write the words from Exercise 2a in a room. Some words can go in a few rooms.

Living room	
Bathroom	*bathtub*
Bedroom	
Kitchen	

Grammar

3 Look at the plan for a new vacation resort and correct the mistakes in the sentences.

> **Ex:** There's one swimming pool.
> *There are two swimming pools.*

1. There isn't a beach near the resort.

   _____

2. There aren't any cafés in the village.

   _____

3. There isn't a place to park your car.

   _____

4. You can't play tennis here.

   _____

4 Write sentences about the village with *there is/ are* (or *there isn't/aren't*).

> **Ex:** (nightclubs) *There aren't any nightclubs in the village.*

1. (a hotel) _____

   _____

2. (spa) _____

   _____

3. (a take-out restaurant) _____

   _____

4. (store) _____

   _____

5. (a tennis court) _____

   _____

6. (a school) _____

   _____

7. (bank) _____

   _____

5 Complete the sentences with the correct form of *there is/are*. (Some sentences are negative.)

> **Ex:** _There is_____ a famous zoo in San Diego.

1. _____ 16 classrooms in our school.

2. _____ any stores near here?

3. _____ a good Chinese take-out in the center of the town.

4. _____ any meat in this meal, so you can eat it.

5. _____ a gym on the ship?

6. _____ a yard with the apartment, but there is a large balcony.

7. _____ any eggs in the refrigerator. Can you get some?

8. _____ a message for you on the answering machine.

9. _____ a concert in the concert hall this Saturday?

10. _____ many answers to that question.

Vocabulary

1a Match the words to make the names of furniture, equipment, and personal possessions. Then write the words. (Some are two or three words.)

_c_ **1.** answering		**a.** player
2. arm		**b.** maker
3. book		~~**c.** machine~~
4. CD		**d.** shelves
5. micro		**e.** washer
6. coffee		**f.** wave
7. dish		**g.** table
8. dining room		**h.** chair

1. _answering machine_
2. _____
3. _____
4. _____
5. _____
6. _____
7. _____
8. _____

b Use 5 words from Exercise 1a to label the pictures.

bookshelf _____

1 _____

2 _____

3 _____

4 _____

2 What is it? Match the words and phrases in the box to the clues.

> bed   sink   stereo   laptop computer
> sofa   ~~stove~~   television   refrigerator

Ex: You can cook meals on it. _stove_

1. You can use it to listen to music. _____
2. You wash dishes in it. _____
3. A few people can sit on it. _____
4. You can watch it. _____
5. You can sleep in it. _____
6. You can put milk in it. _____
7. You send emails from it. _____

Grammar

3 Write sentences with *have/has*.

Ex: Jenny/an apartment in the city
  Jenny has an apartment in the city.

1. I/two brothers

   _____

2. They/a swimming pool

   _____

3. Álvaro/a stereo

   _____

4. We/a new sofa

   _____

5. You/a phone message

   _____

6. I/three TVs

   _____

4 Write sentences as questions (?) or negatives (✗). Use contracted forms for the negatives.

Ex: I have a car. (✗)
  I don't have a car.

  Maria has a dictionary. (?)
  Does Maria have a dictionary?

1. We have a big kitchen. (✗)

   _____

2. Your girlfriend has a car. (?)

   _____

3. She has a DVD player. (✗)

   _____

4. They have a microwave. (?)

   _____

5. You have a watch. (?)

   _____

5 Write questions with the cues. Then write true short answers.

> Ex: your town/theater?
>
> *Does your town have a theater?*
>
> *Yes, it does.*

1. your town/mall?

   _____

   _____

2. your town/airport?

   _____

   _____

3. you/any brothers or sisters?

   _____

   _____

6 Write three sentences about your family with *but* and the correct form of *have*. Use the personal possessions in Exercises 1 and 2.

> Ex: *I have a stove, but I don't have a*
>
> *microwave.*
>
> *My sister has a TV, but she doesn't have*
>
> *a car.*

1. _____

   _____

2. _____

   _____

3. _____

   _____

Communication

7a Read Serena's letter. Circle where she lives.

Dear Pen Pal,

I live in a big house in the country with my husband, Harry. The house has four bedrooms and a big yard. We have two children and three cats—they love the yard. They play in it every day. And we have a garage—I don't have a car but my husband does. I'm an artist, and I work at home. I use one of the bedrooms. It has a big balcony. I can sit on it in the summer and paint the view—it's nice. Harry's a computer programmer. He has three computers. He has a digital camera, and he makes DVDs. In fact we have 40 DVDs now. In the evenings we eat dinner in the kitchen—we don't have a dining room. Then we watch TV in the living room—we have a nice widescreen TV.

Looking forward to hearing from you,

Serena

b Read the letter again and complete the sentences with the correct form of *have* and a number.

> Ex: Their house _has four_ bedrooms.

1. Serena and Harry _____ children.
2. Serena _____ cats.
3. Harry _____ computers.
4. They _____ DVDs.

c Answer the questions with short answers.

> Ex: Does Serena have an apartment in the city?
>
> _No, she doesn't._

1. Do Serena and Harry have any children?

   _____

2. Does Serena have a car?

   _____

3. Does her husband have a car?

   _____

4. Does Serena's house have a balcony?

   _____

5. Do they have a dining room?

   _____

6. Do they have a widescreen TV?

   _____

d Where does Serena live? Check (✓) the correct picture.

A ☐

B ☐

Vocabulary

1a Complete the crossword with adjectives and places, using the clues.

						¹C					
			²L								
	³B				⁴F				
⁵L											
				⁶G					
	H			⁷I			⁸D	
				⁹B		Y		

Clues

- New York is a (2 down) (1 down)—millions of people live there.
- There's a (8 down) (5 across) in my country—there isn't any water in it.
- Redwood National Park is a (3 across) (4 down) in the northern California.
- Kefalonia is a very (6 across) (7 across)—it has a lot of trees.
- Copacabana in Rio de Janeiro is a very (9 across) (3 down)—a lot of people swim there.

b Cross out the word that does not belong.

Ex: river: dangerous ~~modern~~ wide

1. **desert:** hot dry green
2. **mountain:** friendly high cold
3. **city:** dry noisy busy
4. **beach:** popular large modern
5. **island:** green easy tropical
6. **forest:** old busy beautiful
7. **lake:** green dry small

Grammar

2 Write a sentence with your opinion. Use a modifier and the cues.

Ex: Soccer / exciting *Soccer is really exciting.*
or *Soccer isn't very exciting.*

1. Concerts / exciting _____

   _____

2. Our classroom / comfortable _____

   _____

3. Television / relaxing _____

   _____

4. My diet / healthy _____

   _____

5. Video games / interesting _____

   _____

3a Look at the pictures. Use one modifier and one adjective from the box to describe each picture.

Modifiers:	really	~~very~~	not very
	really	very	not very
Adjectives:	big	famous	healthy
	tall	popular	~~wide~~

very wide river

b Now write a sentence to describe each picture in Exercise 3a using the cues.

> Ex: The Amazon/river
>
> *The Amazon is a very wide river.*

1. Police officer/job

   _____

2. The Empire State Building/building

   _____

3. The mini/car

   _____

4. Brad Pitt/actor

   _____

5. Chicken and potatoes/meal

   _____

Writing

4a Read about John and his city. Add capital letters and periods.

>   *J*   *S*   *G*
>
> john is from scotland, in the north of great
>
> britain ‸ he lives in edinburgh, a large city in
>
> the southeast of the country
>
>   there are many interesting places
>
> in edinburgh: museums, theaters, and
>
> restaurants there's an arts festival every year,
>
> and john always goes to it with his friends the
>
> city is also near beautiful lakes and mountains
>
>   john likes edinburgh because it's a very
>
> friendly place he also thinks the city is very
>
> beautiful, but he doesn't like the weather—it's
>
> very cold!

b Find phrases in Exercise 4a that express these ideas. Underline the phrases and then write them in the chart.

How To:	
say where someone lives	*John is from . . .*
describe a country or city	
give someone's opinion	

5 Write an email to a friend about your city or town. Follow these steps.

1. Look at the email on page 53 of your Student Book. How do you start the email?
2. Say where you live.
3. Write two or three sentences to describe your city or town.
4. Give your opinion about your city or town.
5. End the email.

> ● ● ●
>
> _____
>
> Thanks for your email. Here's the
> information about my town. I live in _____
>
> _____
>
> _____
>
> _____
>
> _____
>
> _____
>
> _____
>
> _____
>
> _____
>
> _____
>
> _____
>
> _____
>
> _____
>
> _____

UNIT 6
Around town

Vocabulary

1 Use the clues to complete the crossword.

¹H				²A					
			³C			⁴B			⁵F
	⁶M								
	⁷S								
			⁸A		G				

Clues

1. Doctors and nurses work here.
2. You can live here.
3. You can drink (and sometimes eat) here.
4. You can put your money here.
5. People work here—they make things.
6. You can look at old things here.
7. You can buy all your food and drinks here.
8. You can look at pictures here.

Grammar

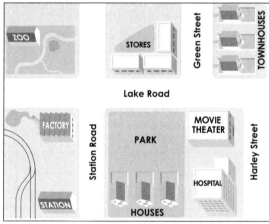

Summertown 2000

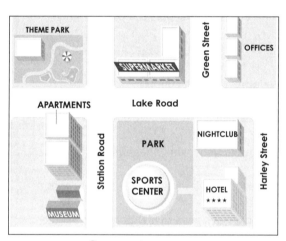

Summertown now

2 Look at the maps. Write sentences about Summertown in 2000.

> Ex: There are offices on Green Street.
> *There were townhouses on Green Street.*

1. There's a theme park on Station Road.
   _____

2. There's a supermarket on Lake Road.
   _____

3. There are apartments on Station Road.
   _____

4. There's a hotel on Harley Street.
   _____

5. There's a sports center in the park.
   _____

3 Write questions about Summertown using the cues. Then answer them.

> Ex: there/supermarket/Lake Road/2000?
> *Was there a supermarket on Lake Road in 2000? No, there wasn't. There were stores.*

1. there/factory/Station Road/2000?
   _____
   _____

2. What/Green Street/2000?
   _____
   _____

3. there/nightclub/Harley Street/2000?
   _____
   _____

4 Angie is a famous singer. Look at her datebook for last week and complete the sentences.

Monday	10		17 clean the house!
Tuesday	11		18 play soccer with boys (afternoon)
Wednesday	12 visit new concert hall 3:00 P.M.		19 **TODAY**
Thursday	13		20
Friday	14 perform at concert hall 8:30 P.M.		21
Saturday	15 open new supermarket 10:30 A.M.		22
Sunday	16 watch DVD concert with Mike, 4:00 P.M.		23

Ex: _Angie visited the new concert hall_ last Wednesday.

1. She _____ _____ last Friday evening.

2. _____ _____ last Saturday morning.

3. _____ _____ on Sunday afternoon.

4. _____ _____ two days ago.

5. _____ _____ yesterday.

5a Complete the story with verbs in the box. Use the simple past.

cook	help	play	relax
~~start~~	walk	watch	work

Luisa's Day

Luisa's day ___started___ at 8:00 A.M. yesterday. She _____ (1.) to work at 9:00, and she _____ (2.) from 9:30 to 4:30. Then she _____ (3.) tennis with a friend from 4:30 to 5:30. At home she _____ (4.) dinner for her family, then she _____ (5.) her son with his school work. In the evening she _____ (6.) a DVD, and she _____ (7.).

b Look at Warren's schedule then write about his day.

start – 6:30 A.M.
walk to bus stop – 7:00
wait for bus – 7:15 to 7:30
work – 8:00 to 4:00
repair cars all day
cook dinner
study – 7:30 to 9:30
listen to music

Warren's Day

Ex: _Warren's day started at 6:30 A.M. yesterday. He_

_____

_____

_____

_____

_____

_____

_____

Reading

6 Put the dialog in the correct order.

_____ B: I decided to have a sandwich in the office, so I stayed at work at lunchtime.

_____ A: But you weren't at home at eight o'clock in the evening.

_1_ A: Where were you yesterday? I wanted to talk to you. I called you at 8:30 in the morning.

_____ B: Yes, I was. I cooked dinner for the children, then I listened to CDs all evening.

_____ B: Oh, I walked to work yesterday, so I wasn't at home at 8:30.

_9_ A: Oh, well, never mind. Can I ask you something now?

_____ B: Well, I visited my friend Rosie in the hospital after work, at about six o'clock, for an hour.

_____ A: But I called you again at lunchtime, and you weren't at home.

_____ A: What about after work? I called you again at five thirty.

Vocabulary

1 Look at the picture. Complete the sentences with the correct prepositions: *in, on, under, behind, between, next to.*

The salad is _*in*_ the sink. The apples are _____ (**1.**) the table, and the potatoes are _____ (**2.**) the chair. The meat is _____ (**3.**) the microwave. The pasta is _____ (**4.**) the microwave, and the eggs are _____ (**5.**) the refrigerator. The cookies are _____ (**6.**) the microwave and the sink. The milk is _____ (**7.**) the refrigerator, and the orange juice is _____ (**8.**) it. The bread is _____ (**9.**) the TV.

2 Read about where the people in the study group sit. Write the names below the desks.

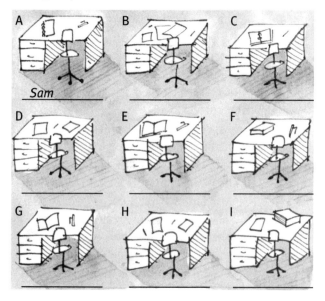

- Steve sits behind Stephanie and next to Susan.
- Sally sits behind Sandy and next to Susan.
- Simon sits in front of Susan and behind Sean.
- Simon sits on the right of Stephanie.
- Sean sits between Sam and Sarah and in front of Simon.
- Sam sits on the left of Sean.

Grammar

3a Write questions in the simple past using the cues.

Ex: you/have/a good vacation?

*Did you have a good vacation?*

1. Where / you / go?

_____

2. you / stay / in a nice place?

_____

3. What / you / do?

_____

4. you / meet / any friends?

_____

5. How long / you / stay?

_____

6. When / you / get home?

_____

b Match questions in Exercise 3a to the answers.

_____ Yes, we did. We stayed in a really good hotel.

_____ Yesterday evening.

__1__ We went to Kyoto, in Japan.

_____ Yes, we did. We know some people there.

_____ We visited lots of museums and galleries.

_____ We stayed for a week.

Communication

4 Use the map below to complete the dialogs.

1. **A:** Excuse me, can you _tell me how to get_ to the art gallery?
   B: Of course. From the station, _____ _____ onto Miller Lane. Then turn right onto Stowe Place and left _____ _____ the road. The art gallery is on the _____ .

2. **A:** Excuse me, do _____ _____ the way to the library?
   B: Yes, it's easy. From the station, turn _____ _____ Miller Lane. The library is at the end of the road, _____ _____ _____ .

3. **A:** Excuse me, is there a hospital near here?
   B: A hospital? Yes, from the station, go straight _____ . Go across the bridge at the end of Station Road and _____ _____ onto Park Lane. The hospital is _____ _____ _____ .

4. **A:** Excuse me, can you _____ _____ _____ _____ to the school?
   B: Yes. From the station, go _____ on Station Road to Hillfield Avenue. Turn _____ . Go down two _____ . The school is on the left.

Writing

5a Write directions from the station.

1. Excuse me, can you tell me the way to the movie theater?
   Yes, of course. From the station, _____ _____ _____ _____ _____ _____

2. Excuse me, do you know the way to the supermarket?
   Yes, there's a supermarket on Hillfield Avenue. You go straight on Station Road _____ _____ _____ _____ _____

3. Excuse me, is there a bank near here?
   Yes, there is. From the station, _____ _____ _____ _____ _____

b Choose a place near your home: library, school, store, or hospital. Write directions from your home to one of these places.

_____
_____
_____
_____
_____
_____
_____
_____

Reading

1a Read the article quickly and answer the question.

How long was Lewis and Clark's journey? _____ years

LEWIS AND CLARK

Meriwether Lewis and William Clark are famous American explorers. In 1804 President Thomas Jefferson wanted a map of the western United States because at that time people didn't know the area west of the Mississippi River. Lewis and Clark started from St. Louis in 1804 with 30 men and a Native American woman, Sacagawea. The weather was very bad, and it was difficult to travel. They stayed for the winter with a tribe of Native Americans.

After the winter they traveled over the Rocky Mountains. Various Native Americans helped them find the Pacific Ocean at the end of 1805. They discovered many new rivers and mountains, and they measured everything for their maps. They started back at the start of 1806, and they finished their journey at the end of the year. They traveled 8,000 miles and discovered that North America was a very large place.

b Read the article again and put the events in order. (Use a dictionary to check any new words.)

_____ They stayed the winter with the Native Americans.

_____ They finished their journey to the Pacific Ocean.

__1__ The president wanted a map of the western US.

_____ They started back in 1806.

_____ They traveled over the Rocky Mountains.

_____ Lewis and Clark started from St. Louis.

_____ The weather was very bad.

c Now answer these questions.

Ex: Why did the president want a map of the western United States?

Because people didn't know the area
west of the Mississippi River.

1. How many people were there on the journey?

_____

2. What did they measure?

_____

3. What did they discover?

_____

Grammar

2 Use the cues to write negative sentences in the simple past.

Ex: Christopher Columbus/invent/the compass

Christopher Columbus didn't invent
the compass.

Charles Darwin/be American

Charles Darwin wasn't American.

1. William Shakespeare/write/*Don Quixote*

_____

2. My great-grandparents/own/a car

_____

3. Queen Elizabeth I/be/married

_____

4. We/have/cell phones in the 1970s

_____

5. My father/go/to the university

_____

6. He/study/foreign languages at school

_____

7. In ancient times people/eat/a lot of food and they/be/tall _____

_____

Vocabulary

3   Use the pictures to complete the puzzle with forms of transportation.

Crossword letters (given): C, T R, T A, B I, P A N, B S

4   Write true sentences with the words in the chart.

1.	The minivan		an invention	in New York.
2.	China's *China Star* and Japan's *Shinkansen*	is are was were	popular	family car.
3.	Yellow taxis		high-speed	of the 19th century.
4.	The railways		a useful	trains.

1. *The minivan is a useful family car.*
2. _____
3. _____
4. _____

Writing

5a Think about a great trip from your past. Make notes to answer these questions.

1. Where did you go?
    _____

2. Who was with you on the trip?
    _____

3. When was it?
    _____

4. When did it start and finish?
    _____

5. What did you visit?
    _____

6. How did you travel?
    _____

7. Where did you stay?
    _____

8. How long was the trip?
    _____

9. What did you like?
    _____

10. What didn't you like?
    _____

11. Why was it "a great trip"?
    _____

b   Write a 100-word paragraph about your trip on a separate piece of paper.

c   Check your paragraph for grammar, spelling, and punctuation mistakes, then rewrite it.

Grammar
Count and noncount nouns

1   Put the nouns in the box in the correct column in the chart.

> salad   receipt   dishwasher
> rice   money   mayonnaise
> bread   cookie   armchair

Count nouns	Noncount nouns

How much?/How many?; a/an/ some/any

2   Circle the correct choice.

1. I'd like *some/any* cheese, please.
2. How *much/many* meat do you eat every week?
3. Is there *some/any* milk in the refrigerator?
4. Jack always takes *a/some* cream in his coffee.
5. How *much/many* students are there in the class?
6. I can't see you now. I don't have *some/any* time.
7. Do you have *any/a* DVD player?
8. How *much/many* bathrooms are there?
9. Please give me *some/a* carton of orange juice.
10. Here's *some/any* money.

Object pronouns

3   Complete the sentences with an object pronoun.

1. That's my coffee. It's for _____ .
2. It's John's dictionary. Please give it to _____ .
3. A: Is that Maria and Rey? B: Yes, it's _____ .
4. That's Eddie's new car. Do you like _____ ?
5. Your girlfriend's on the phone. She wants to speak to _____ .
6. A: That's Sophie's sister. B: Yes, I know _____ .
7. That's my credit card. Please give it to _____ .
8. Tony likes our house. He always stays with _____ when he comes to London.
9. A: Have some fries with your burger. B: No, thanks. I don't like _____ .
10. A: Is that Sarah in class? B: Yes, that's _____ .

there is/there are

4   Complete the dialog with a form of *there is/ there are*.

A: I think I'd like to take the apartment. _____ (**1.**) furniture in the living room?

B: Well, _____ (**2.**) a big sofa.

A: _____ (**3.**) a dining room table?

B: Yes, _____ (**4.**), and _____ (**5.**) four chairs.

A: Oh, good. _____ (**6.**) a coffee table?

B: No, _____ (**7.**).

A: Oh, and what about a television, or a stereo?

B: No, _____ (**8.**) any electronics.

Modifiers

5   Circle the correct modifier. Then write sentences.

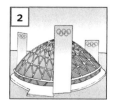

Ex: *not very/*(really)   unhappy/my sister/today
    My sister is really unhappy today.

1. *not very/really*   late/we
_____

2. *very/not very*   the new sports center/modern
_____

3. *really/pretty*   my lunch/unhealthy
_____

4. *really/pretty*   this movie/boring
_____

5. *very/not very*   well-equipped/the kitchen
_____

have/has

6 Write questions using the cues. Then write short answers. (✓) = Yes, (✗) = No.

Ex: Alex/a DVD player (✗)
Does Alex have a DVD player? No, he
doesn't.

1. you/a microwave? (✗)

   _____

   _____

2. Sarah/a credit card? (✓)

   _____

   _____

3. your parents/a big yard? (✗)

   _____

   _____

4. we/any cookies? (✗)

   _____

   _____

5. the dog/any food? (✓)

   _____

   _____

Simple past

7a Write the simple past forms of these verbs.

1. be _____   6. travel _____
2. decide _____   7. visit _____
3. marry _____   8. want _____
4. open _____   9. work _____
5. stop _____   10. help _____

b Complete the story with simple past verbs from Exercise 7a. Use the negative if you see (not).

My father was only 16 when he _stopped_ going to school. He was unhappy at school, and he _____ (1. not) to go to college—he wanted to go to work. He _____ (2.) in a factory for five years, but he still wasn't very happy, so he _____ (3.) to leave the factory and see some of the world. He _____ (4.) to Peru and he stayed there for ten years. He _____ (5.) my mother, but they decided to come back to Canada to start a family. At that time, it was very unusual to have a Peruvian wife, and people _____ (6. not) very friendly to them at first. My parents _____ (7.) a Peruvian restaurant and a lot of people _____ (8.) it and enjoyed the food. So I was very happy when I was a child—with loving parents and a lot of money!

c Read the story again. Correct the sentences.

Ex: The father stopped school when he was 14.
He didn't stop going to school when he
was 14. He stopped when he was 16.

1. He went to college.

   _____

   _____

2. He stayed at the factory for ten years.

   _____

   _____

3. He married a woman in Africa.

   _____

   _____

4. The writer's parents opened a factory.

   _____

   _____

Vocabulary

8a Complete the chart with words from the box.

bed	library	dining room
hall	bicycle	post office
desk	kitchen	pharmacy
table	bathroom	newsstand
boat	motorcycle	
train	bookshelf	

Rooms	Furniture	Places in a town	Transportation

b Complete the sentences with words from the chart.

1. We prepare food in the _____ .
2. We can take a _____ through the Panama Canal.
3. I want to get a book at the _____ .
4. We have a shower in our _____ .
5. I do my homework at my _____ .
6. I bought a newspaper at the _____?
7. Please put your books on the _____ .

Vocabulary

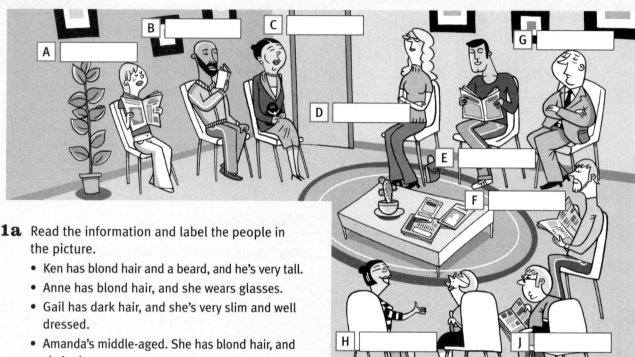

1a Read the information and label the people in the picture.

- Ken has blond hair and a beard, and he's very tall.
- Anne has blond hair, and she wears glasses.
- Gail has dark hair, and she's very slim and well dressed.
- Amanda's middle-aged. She has blond hair, and she's short.
- Henry has a beard and is bald.
- Surinda's very friendly. She has dark hair.
- Melanie's young and pretty. She has blond hair.
- Jeremy's bald.
- Alvaro's handsome and tan. He has dark hair.
- Stefan's pretty heavy. He has blond hair.

b Complete these sentences about the picture with numbers or adjectives.

> Ex: *Three* people wear glasses.

1. Five people have _____ hair.
2. _____ people have beards.
3. _____ people have dark hair.
4. Two men are _____.

c Complete the sentences with words from Exercise 1a.

1. I wear _____ when I read.
2. It was very sunny last week, so now I am _____.
3. Delia's very tall, but her parents are _____.
4. Do you think Matt Damon is _____?
5. Young female movie stars are often very _____.
6. My children are very _____—they talk to everyone.

2 Complete the sentences with adjectives that describe the people.

1. Sam doesn't like going to parties and meeting new people. He's _____.
2. Mrs. Barrett is 98. She's very _____.
3. We like our teacher. She's really _____.

3 Write a sentence describing each of these people.

1. A member of your family

_____

2. A famous movie star or pop star

_____

3. Your best friend

_____

4 Match the adjectives to their opposites. Use a dictionary.

_____	1. comfortable	a.	tiny
_____	2. huge	b.	modern
_____	3. quick	c.	good
_____	4. early	d.	exact
_____	5. married	e.	interesting
_____	6. bad	f.	late
_____	7. old-fashioned	g.	poor
_____	8. boring	h.	uncomfortable
_____	9. rich	i.	single
_____	10. approximate	j.	slow

Grammar

5 Match the <u>underlined</u> words to the words below.

_____ swimming pool   _____ CDs

_1__ shopping center   _____ salad

_____ sports club

There is a big shopping center in our town, and there is a small <u>one</u> (**1.**) near our house. We go there every Saturday morning. I go to the supermarket and get the food. My husband usually goes to the bookstore and buys CDs. He likes classical <u>ones</u> (**2.**). Then we have lunch. I usually have a small salad, and my husband has a large <u>one</u> (**3.**). In the afternoon we go to the sports club. It's a modern <u>one</u> (**4.**) with two swimming pools. My husband uses the indoor pool, and I use the outdoor <u>one</u> (**5.**).

6 Rewrite the sentences using *one* or *ones*.

Ex: My girlfriend has a car, but I don't have a car.
    My girlfriend has a car but I don't have one.

1. I like hot places, but Sally likes cold places.

   _____

   _____

2. Can I have six large salads and two small salads, please? _____

   _____

3. We have three bedrooms—I sleep in the big bedroom. _____

   _____

4. Are they the blue chairs, the red chairs, or the yellow chairs? _____

   _____

5. The first apartment has a balcony, and the second apartment has a yard. _____

   _____

Writing

7a Fill in the blanks (a and b) and write short answers to the questions below.

(a) _____ Jenna,

Thanks for your last letter. It was really funny! I started my International Studies course at the university last month. My first course is Spanish. I'm in the beginners' class. Our teacher is nice. She's middle-aged, and she comes from Toledo. She's very friendly. My classmates are very nice. There are three girls and five boys in the class. Two of the boys are only 18 but the others are the same age as me—19.

The lessons are difficult, but they're very interesting. I like the grammar and the listening exercises. I do two hours of homework every day. I usually work in the university study center because there are a lot of dictionaries and some computers with really useful language programs. In the evening I go out with some of my classmates—we have a lot of fun! Give my love to Mom and Dad and write again soon.

(b) _____,
Barbara

1. Who is the letter to? _____
2. Who is the letter from? _____
3. Are Jenna and Barbara sisters or friends?

   _____
4. Where does Barbara study? _____
5. Where does Barbara's teacher come from?

   _____
6. How many students are in the Spanish class?

   _____
7. Why does Barbara work in the study center?

   _____
8. What does Barbara want Jenna to do?

   _____

b Write a letter to a close relative (brother, sister, etc.) or friend on a separate piece of paper. Tell him or her about your school, your English class, your teacher, and classmates. Use Barbara's letter as a model.

Grammar

A | This apartment belongs to you and your best friend.

D | Your brother's bicycle.

B | Your parents' car.

C | Your motorcycle.

E | Your sister's car.

1 Match A–E in the picture to the statements below.

_C_ **1.** It's mine. _____ **2.** It's his. _____ **3.** It's hers. _____ **4.** It's ours. _____ **5.** It's theirs.

2 Circle the correct choice.

Ex: That's not your book, it's _me_/_mine_.

1. Can I use _your/yours_ car this evening?

2. We can hear _theirs/their_ television in our living room.

3. Take one of the pens, they're _ours/our_.

4. Is this dictionary _your/yours_?

5. Don't drink that coffee, it's _hers/her_.

6. You can use _mine/my_ umbrella.

7. Are those _her/hers_ sneakers?

8. The present isn't for us. It's _theirs/their_.

3 Replace the underlined phrases with the expressions in the box.

is theirs	isn't ours	isn't yours
~~isn't mine~~	are ours	is ours
is mine	aren't his	belongs to you

Ex: You can't use that computer. It <u>doesn't belong to me</u>. _isn't mine_

1. I think this book <u>is yours</u>. _____

2. That cell phone <u>belongs to me</u>. _____

3. The house on the left <u>belongs to Alice and her husband</u>. _____

4. The big present <u>is for us</u>. _____

5. The television <u>doesn't belong to us</u>. It belongs to my parents. _____

6. Don't drink that cup of coffee. It <u>isn't for you</u>, it's for Mauro. _____

7. Those vacation photos <u>belong to us</u>. _____

8. The chairs <u>aren't my brother's</u>. They belong to his wife. _____

4 Complete the story with the words in the box.

mine	his	hers	ours	yours	~~theirs~~

I live in a large apartment with my sister. It belongs to our parents. The furniture doesn't belong to me and my sister—it's all _theirs_, too. But the television and stereo are _____ (**1.**)—we bought them together last year. We both have cell phones: _____ (**2.**) is a smart phone, and my sister's is a slider. We use them a lot, but _____ (**3.**) isn't very good because it doesn't have a camera. My phone has a camera and it plays music. My sister's boyfriend has a really good phone. He can use _____ (**4.**) when he travels because it works in lots of different countries. Do you have a cell phone? Can you use _____ (**5.**) in different countries?

Communication

5a Complete the conversation with possessive pronouns.

Ana: Ah, Phil. You have the food.

Phil: Yes. Here we are. Now, let's see. The chicken sandwich, that's __*yours*__, Ana.

Ana: No, it isn't _____ (1.). That's for Darren. He wanted chicken.

Phil: Right, sorry. The chicken sandwich is _____ (2.).

Ana: Yes. And I wanted the tuna salad sandwich. It's _____ (3.).

Phil: OK. Is the salad _____ (4.), too?

Ana: No, that's for Sylvia.

Phil: Yes, that's _____ (5.). And the cups of coffee?

Ana: They're for Dave and Joe.

Phil: Right. And the burgers are _____ (6.), too, I think . . .

Ana: Yes, they are. What about the orange juice and the bag of chips? Did you want them? Are they _____ (7.)?

Phil: Yes, they're _____ (8.).

b Read the conversation again. Who are the food and drinks for? Complete the chart with checks (✓).

	Phil	Ana	Dave and Joe	Sylvia	Darren
Orange juice					
Cups of coffee					
Chicken sandwich					
Tuna salad sandwich					
Burgers					
Salad					
Bag of chips					

Vocabulary

6 Answer the questions. Write the ordinal numbers as words.

> Ex: What date is one month before March 5th?
> __*February fifth*__

1. What date is two months after September 18th? _____
2. What month comes after May? _____
3. What day comes between Tuesday and Thursday? _____
4. What day comes after Friday? _____
5. What date is three months before October 22nd? _____
6. July 1st is Monday. What day is July 7th? _____
7. What date is three weeks after August 3rd? _____

7 Write the underlined dates as words.

> Ex: Independence Day in the US is on 7/4.
> __*July fourth*__

1. 12/25 is Christmas Day.
   _____
2. William Shakespeare's birthday is 4/23.
   _____
3. St. Patrick's Day, 3/17, is a holiday in Ireland.
   _____
4. 12/26 is a holiday in Great Britain, Canada, and Australia. _____
5. Pedro Álvares Cabral landed in Brazil on 4/22, 1500. _____
6. My birthday is 10/19. _____
7. The Second World War started on 9/3, 1939.
   _____

Reading

1 Read the article quickly. What is it about? Circle the answer.

1. a new type of dollar bill
2. a man who tried to steal something
3. a problem with the police

It's a crazy world!

A man was in a Springfield police station last night after he tried to steal a 100,000 dollar bill from a car.

The man, a 28-year-old local, noticed the bill inside a parked car. The thief broke into the car and took the bill, but people in the street saw him and called the police. The police arrived quickly, caught the man, and put him in a police car.

Unfortunately for the man, the bill wasn't even a real bill—US bills only go up to 10,000, not 100,000. The bill was in fact an advertisement for a local business. The business made the fake 100,000 bills to advertise a competition—people could win $100,000 as the top prize in the competition. The thief didn't understand that the bill wasn't real!

2 Match the words to their meanings.

_____ **1.** steal   **a.** false, not real

_____ **2.** thief   **b.** sadly

_____ **3.** broke into   **c.** went into a house/car to take something

_____ **4.** unfortunately

_____ **5.** fake   **d.** a person who takes things and doesn't ask

     e. to take something from someone and not ask

3a Answer the questions.

Ex: What did the man see?

A fake $100,000 bill

1. Did he know it was fake? _____
2. What did he do? _____
_____

3. How did the police catch him? _____
_____

4. Who made the bills? Why? _____
_____

b Read the article again. Put the events in the correct order.

_____ The police caught the man.

_1_ A business made some fake bills as advertisements.

_____ They put him in their police car.

_____ He broke into the car and tried to steal it.

_____ A man noticed one of the fake bills in a car.

Grammar

4 Complete the chart with the simple past form of these irregular verbs.

	Base form	Simple past form
1.	be	_was/were_
2.	leave	_____
3.	buy	_____
4.	break	_____
5.	take	_____
6.	see	_____
7.	swim	_____
8.	feel	_____
9.	catch	_____
10.	put	_____
11.	make	_____
12.	get	_____

5 Rewrite the sentences using the simple past.

Ex: Thieves often break into the bank.

Thieves broke into the bank

again last night.

1. We catch the bus to work every morning.

_____

yesterday morning.

2. Don and Eva see their grandchildren once a week.

_____

last Sunday.

3. Mom makes fantastic chocolate cookies.

_____

for the party last weekend.

4. Xavier takes hundreds of photos on every vacation.

_____

on his last vacation.

5. I swim across the lake in 20 minutes.

_____

when I was a child.

6. Alicia puts a lot of sugar in her coffee.

_____

in her coffee yesterday.

7. They aren't very happy about the weather.

_____

about the weather on their vacation.

8. The train usually leaves on time.

_____

late yesterday morning.

6a Write questions about the past with the cues.

1. When/you/go to bed/last night/?

_____

2. Where/you/be/yesterday/?

_____

3. What/you/buy/last weekend/?

_____

4. Who/you/meet/three months ago/?

_____

5. What movies/you/see/last year/?

_____

6. How/you/feel/five years ago/?

_____

b Answer the questions in Exercise 6a. Write true answers about yourself.

1. Last night _____

_____.

2. Yesterday _____

_____.

3. Last weekend _____

_____.

4. Three months ago _____

_____.

5. Last year _____

_____.

6. Five years ago _____

_____.

Dressing right

LESSON **1**

Vocabulary

1 Find clothing words and adjectives in the chains.

1 (JACKE~~T~~)SHIR~~T~~IGHTOPANTS

clothing words: _jacket_ _T-shirt_ _____
_____ adjective: _____

2 DRESSHORTSHOESCARFORMAL

clothing words: _____ _____ _____
_____ adjective: _____

3 WARMATCHINGLOVESUITIE

clothing words: _____ _____ _____
adjectives: _____ _____

2 Complete the chart with words in the box. Some words can go in two columns.

~~coat~~	gloves	sweater	jeans	suit
scarf	shorts	sneakers	T-shirt	tie

Summer	Winter	Formal	Casual
	coat		

3 Label the pictures using an adjective in the box and a clothing word.

formal	loose	~~fashionable~~
tight	thick	light

Grammar

4 Put the words in the correct order to make sentences.

Ex: in the Sahara desert/It/rains/never
   It never rains in the Sahara desert.

1. wear/a suit/I/hardly ever/to work
   _____

2. sometimes/Mrs. Gladstone/late/is
   _____

3. my parents/often/We/visit/on the weekend
   _____

4. to Mexico/They/in the summer/go/usually
   _____

5. my mother/on Saturdays/always/I/call
   _____

5 Rewrite the sentences with adverbs of frequency.

Ex: Dimitri goes to the gym four times a week.
   Dimitri often goes to the gym.

1. Jason doesn't smoke.
   _____

2. I go to the theater once a year.
   _____

3. They watch the TV news every day.
   _____

4. Jennifer wears a dress once or twice a week.
   _____

5. From Monday to Saturday he gets up at 7:00 A.M.
   _____

fashionable jacket   2 _____

1 _____   3 _____   5 _____

Reading

A

Dear Alison,

Can you give me some ___advice___?
I work in a bank. I _____ (**1.**)
a suit and a tie and nice shoes.
The bank is near my house, and
I usually walk to work. In the
summer it is very hot, and I feel very
_____ (**2.**) in my formal clothes
when I walk to the bank. What
_____ (**3.**) I do?

Jason Grey

B

Dear Alison,

_____ (**4.**) help me? I work at
a sports club and I usually wear
sneakers, shorts, and a T-shirt. In
the morning I _____ (**5.**) help
in the gym, but in the afternoon
I sometimes work in the office.
My co-workers in the office say
I _____ (**6.**) look nice in my
shorts and T-shirt. How can I wear
comfortable clothes for the gym
and look _____ (**7.**) in the
office? What do you suggest?

Sophia Antrim

Answer

Comfortable casual clothes
can be fashionable. But
don't wear a T-shirt and
shorts in the office. Wear
_____ (**8.**) cotton pants
and clean sneakers. Wear a
T-shirt, but get a nice cotton
top and _____ (**9.**) it on
when you go into the office.
You can take it off when
you work in the gym.

6a Complete the sentences in the letters with words and expressions in the box.

don't	put	~~advice~~	uncomfortable
wear	nice	Can you	
can	light	usually	

b Read the letters and the answer. Is the answer for Letter A or B? _____

c Write questions for these answers.

Ex: _Where does Jason work?_

In a bank.

1. _____

A suit and a tie and nice shoes.

2. _____

He walks.

3. _____

In a sports club.

4. _____

In the morning.

5. _____

She doesn't look nice.

Writing

7 Read the information and write an email to Dana.

Next month you begin a new office job at SystemPro
Incorporated, a big American computer company in
your hometown. You don't know very much about the
company.

You want to know about these things:
- clothes
- personal phone calls and emails
- smoking
- lunch breaks

Dana, a co-worker from your old job, now works for
SystemPro Incorporated. You want her advice.

_____
_____
_____
_____
_____
_____
_____
_____
_____
_____
_____

Communication

1 Look at the people in the picture. Match the activities to the people.

Ex: __I__ She's waiting at the check-in desk.

_____ **1.** He's eating a burger.

_____ **2.** She's reading and laughing.

_____ **3.** He's shouting.

_____ **4.** She's carrying a suitcase.

_____ **5.** They're wearing suits.

_____ **6.** She's feeling unhappy.

_____ **7.** He's walking away from man F.

_____ **8.** She's smoking.

_____ **9.** He's eating a sandwich.

2a A police detective is at the airport. He is looking for Ron Tyler, a thief, and his gang. Read the conversation on page 53. Which letter is the police officer? _____

b Read the conversation again and write the letter for each person.

Ex: __F__ Ron Tyler

_____ **1.** Leanne Tyler, his wife

_____ **2.** Mikey Tyler, Ron's son

_____ **3.** Big Dave

_____ **4.** Tracey, Mikey's girlfriend

_____ **5.** Hayley, Ron's daughter

A: Where are you, Brian?

B: I'm at the airport. I'm watching those famous thieves—the Tyler Gang.

A: Oh, good. Are they all there?

B: I think so, but I don't know all of them. I can see Ron Tyler—he's talking on his cell phone. He's shouting. He isn't happy!

A: Is his wife there?

B: Leanne? Yes, she is. She's looking at a magazine at the bookstore. She's laughing.

A: What about Ron's son, Mikey?

B: Is he big and ugly?

A: Yes, that's Mikey!

B: I see him. He's eating a burger. Wait a minute. He's meeting someone . . . yes, a young woman. She's arriving now. She's short and pretty. She's carrying a large suitcase.

A: That's Mikey's girlfriend, Tracey. A big suitcase . . . interesting. Is Ron's daughter Hayley there?

B: Yes, she's waiting at the check-in desk. She's smoking. She looks confused.

A: Hayley's always confused. What about her husband, Big Dave? He's the dangerous one . . .

B: Oh, yes. Oh, no! He's watching me . . . now he's walking towards me . . . I'm going!

Grammar

3a Write about the people in the picture. What are they doing?

Ex: **A.** Leanne _is reading a magazine. She's_ _laughing._

B. Tracey _____

_____

C. Mikey _____

_____

D. _____

_____

E. _____

_____

F. Ron Tyler _____

_____

G. Brian _____

_____

H. Big Dave _____

_____

I. Hayley _____

_____

J. _____

_____

b Write questions with the cues. Then answer the questions.

Ex: Tracey/carry/a small bag?

Is Tracey carrying a small bag? No, she _isn't. She's carrying a large suitcase._

1. Mikey/wear/jeans?

_____

_____

2. Mikey/eat/a sandwich?

_____

_____

3. Hayley/smoke?

_____

_____

4. Big Dave/wear/a coat?

_____

_____

5. Leanne/feel/unhappy?

_____

_____

4a Complete the chart.

	Adjective	Adverb
1.	bad	_badly_
2.	_____	carelessly
3.	close	_____
4.	comfortable	_____
5.	_____	well
6.	happy	_____
7.	_____	fast
8.	quick	_____
9.	sad	_____
10.	_____	strangely

b Underline and correct the five mistakes. Check (✓) the correct sentence.

Ex: Are you sitting comfortable? _comfortably_

Francisco always does his work carefully. _✓_

1. Don't run so fast! _____

2. You look sadly today—what's wrong? _____

3. Marina always talks very loud. _____

4. You sing very good. Are you a singer? _____

5. Kevin is a strangely person. _____

6. The children are playing very quiet in their room.

_____

Vocabulary

1 Look at the map. Complete the sentences with the weather words in the box.

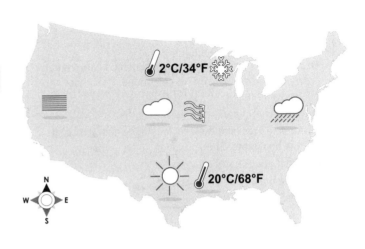

> ~~foggy~~   warm   sunny   windy
> snowing   cold   raining   cloudy

Ex: It's _foggy_____ in the west.

1. It's _____ and _____ in the middle of the country.

2. It's _____ and _____ in the north.

3. It's _____ and _____ in the south.

4. It's _____ in the east.

Reading

2a Read the article about the weather and our health. Complete the chart with checks (✓) .

	Good for us	Bad for us	Good and bad
The sun			
Hot weather			
Cold weather			

b Read the article again. Mark the sentences true (*T*) or false (*F*).

Ex: _F___ It is healthy to have a tan.

_____ 1. Hot weather is often good for people with depression.

_____ 2. The cold can affect older people badly.

_____ 3. People can get tired and sleep badly in hot weather.

_____ 4. Many people think cold mountain air is depressing.

c Complete the chart with nouns and adjectives from the article in Exercise 2a.

	Nouns	Adjectives
	health	healthy
1.	importance	_____
2.	_____	tan
3.	_____	depressed
4.	sickness	_____
5.	darkness	_____

Weather wise

Can the weather really affect our health and our moods? Read and find out!

The sun

● The sun can be good for us. It gives us vitamin D—this is very important for young people when they are growing.

● But the sun can also be bad for us. A lot of sun can hurt our skin very badly—a tan really is not healthy.

Hot weather

● Hot weather can be bad for us. We lose water from our bodies, and that can be dangerous. It's a good idea to drink a lot of water when it's hot.

● Very hot weather can also affect our moods. In hot weather people often get tired, have headaches, and sleep badly. It can also affect people with depression.

Cold weather

● A lot of older people have problems when it's very cold because their body temperature falls quickly, and they become sick.

● Some people become very depressed in cold, dark weather. They can't sleep, and they don't eat a lot.

● Cold weather can be good for us, too. People often feel very strong and healthy in the mountains because the cold air is very clean and relaxing.

Communication

3 Read the conversation below and find the following information.

Ex: a sentence giving an opinion

I think it looks awful.

1. a question asking for an opinion

_____

2. an agreement

_____

3. a disagreement

_____

Anna:	Hello, Carmen. <u>What are you doing</u> (**1.**) here?
Carmen:	Hi. <u>I'm waiting</u> (**2.**) to go on the sun tanning bed. <u>I'm trying</u> (**3.**) to get a good tan before we go on vacation.
Anna:	Really? Why?
Carmen:	Well, I think it looks awful if you're the only pale person on the beach. Don't you think so?
Anna:	Well, no, I'm not sure. It isn't healthy to have a tan, you know.
Carmen:	Oh, I agree that you need to be careful. <u>I always spend</u> (**4.**) just ten minutes on the tanning bed. <u>I never stay</u> (**5.**) for very long. You aren't here for the a tan, then, Anna?
Anna:	Oh, no. <u>I'm meeting</u> (**6.**) my fitness instructor—there he is.
Carmen:	Oh, <u>do you often come</u> (**7.**) to the gym?
Anna:	Yes, <u>I use the gym</u> (**8.**) three or four times a week.
Carmen:	Wow—you're very fit!

Grammar

4 Look at the <u>underlined</u> phrases in the conversation in Exercise 3. Write the numbers of the phrases on the correct line.

Actions happening now: _1,_____

Actions that happen regularly: _4,_____

5 Write sentences about Jason. Use the cues in the boxes and the pictures.

Jason lives in the city, and he works in a department store. Every day . . .

> ~~take the bus to work~~   sell men's clothes
> play computer games
> eat a burger with friends

Ex: _He takes the bus to work._____

1. _____
2. _____
3. _____

This week Jason is on vacation. What's he doing?

> ~~sunbathe on the beach~~   swim in the ocean
> play soccer on the beach
> eat fish at a restaurant

Ex: _He's sunbathing on the beach._____

4. _____
5. _____
6. _____

LESSON 1

Reading

1a Look quickly at the article. Circle what is it about.

   a. newspapers   **b.** media use   **c.** the Internet

People in the US like their local newspapers and local TV news. But recently new technology is changing Americans' media habits.

According to a recent Gallup poll, about 40% of people in the US read a local newspaper every day. But that number is down from a decade ago when 53% said they read a local paper daily. The number of people who get their news from local TV news is also decreasing, down from 57 to 51%.

Meanwhile, and not surprisingly, a growing number of people use the Internet as their source of news. The Gallup poll found that 31% of all people in the US check the news on the Internet at least once a day. That's a 24% increase from 7% ten years ago. Cable news networks, such as CNN and MSNBC, are also enjoying more popularity. The poll found that 40% of people watch the news on these and other cable networks every day, up from 21% ten years ago—an increase of 19%.

Interestingly, however, the poll also found that more than half of the people interviewed—57%—say they don't have much or any trust in the media. That's even higher than the 43% who said the media wasn't trustworthy 10 years ago, and a higher percentage than any number recorded in the last 40 years.

b Read the article. Then match the words to the meanings.

_____ **1.** habit

_____ **2.** poll

_____ **3.** decade

_____ **4.** meanwhile

_____ **5.** trust

   a. at the same time

   b. something you do every day

   c. a report about people's opinions or activities

   d. confidence

   e. ten years

c Complete the chart with information from the article.

Percent of people who . . .	Now	10 years ago
read a local newspaper every day		
watch local news on TV every day		
read the news on the Internet every day		
watch cable TV news every day		
don't trust the media		

d Use the article and the chart to answer the questions.

   1. What are some examples of media?

   _____

   2. What kinds of media were popular for news ten years ago?

   _____

   3. What two kinds of media are increasingly popular as sources of news today?

   _____

   4. How do most people feel about the media?

   _____

Grammar

2a Look at the chart in Exercise 1c. Then complete the sentences.

1. Newspapers are _____ popular _____ they were ten years ago.

2. Today local TV news is _____ popular _____ newspapers.

3. Today Internet news is _____ popular _____ it was ten years ago.

4. Cable TV news was _____ popular _____ local news ten years ago.

b Use the words in the box and the cues to compare media. Write two sentences.

good	exciting	trustworthy
bad	detailed	expensive
cheap	convenient	interesting
fast	visual	popular

Ex: local newspaper/local TV news
The local newspaper is better than the local TV news. But the local TV news is more popular.

1. newspaper/radio

_____
_____
_____

2. the Internet/apps

_____
_____
_____

3. cable news/local news

_____
_____
_____

4. movies on TV/movies in theaters

_____
_____
_____

5. flying in an airplane/taking a train

_____
_____
_____

3a Find pairs of opposite adjectives.

~~formal~~	clean	early
loose	hot	tight
	messy	quiet
late	unhealthy	noisy
easy	cold	
~~casual~~		difficult
	healthy	

formal—casual _____   _____
_____   _____
_____   _____
_____   _____

b Use adjectives from Exercise 3a to compare these people and things.

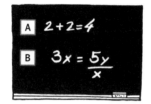

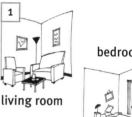

bedroom
living room
Emma
Caroline

Egypt
Greenland
Harriet   Harry

Ex: *Problem A is easier than problem B.* or
Problem B is more difficult than problem A.

1. _____
_____

2. _____
_____

3. _____
_____

4. _____
_____

Vocabulary

1a Find seven more types of movies. Two types are two words and one type has two different names.

C	T	M	U	S	I	C	A	L	Y	D
B	A	G	S	C	I	E	N	C	E	F
A	R	D	T	Y	K	O	Q	H	W	I
N	D	F	V	A	B	J	X	O	S	C
I	C	O	M	E	D	Y	Z	R	G	T
M	W	C	M	L	N	T	U	R	O	I
A	E	D	C	A	R	T	O	O	N	O
T	A	C	T	I	O	N	U	R	N	N
E	L	O	V	E	S	T	O	R	Y	V
D	J	D	T	H	R	I	L	L	E	R

b Write the movie types from Exercise 1a.

Ex: It's a funny movie. a _comedy_

1. Girls and boys meet and fall in love.
   a(n)_____
2. It's scary. Awful things happen.
   a(n) _____ movie
3. The people aren't real. They're pictures.
   a(n) _____ movie
4. The story is exciting. There's lots of movement.
   a(n) _____ or _____ movie
5. There's singing and dancing in this.
   a(n) _____
6. People sometimes live in space in this type of movie. a(n) _____ movie
7. You don't know the answer before the end.
   a(n) _____

Grammar

2 Each sentence contains a mistake with the superlative. Correct the mistakes.

Ex: Mr. Sanders is ~~the most rich~~ man in our town.
   Mr. Sanders is the richest man in our town.

1. Salima is the most best student in the class.

   _____

2. The Pacific is the bigger ocean in the world.

   _____

3. My sister's baby is newest member of our family.

   _____

4. I bought the most cheap printer in the store.

   _____

5. Ali is the most attractivest girl in the group.

   _____

3 Write comparisons using adjectives in the box.

> heavy   intelligent   ~~rich~~
> young   romantic

Ex: Martin has $30,000, Justin has $70,000, and Frank has $55,000.
   Justin is the richest man.

1. Sarah's baby is three months old, Stacy's baby is four months old, and Lauren's baby is two months old.

   _____

2. Dave, Kari, and Luis are all in school. Dave got 86 percent on his exams, Kari got 74 percent, and Luis got 92 percent.

   _____

3. Christa's weight is 131 pounds, Jan's weight is 112 pounds, and Andy's weight is 153 pounds.

   _____

4. Paul buys his girlfriend flowers on her birthday. William buys his girlfriend flowers every month. Peter buys his girlfriend flowers once a week.

   _____

4 Write sentences using the cues and *is, are, was,* or *were.*

Ex: rich/country in South America/Chile
   The richest country in South America is
   Chile.

1. young/tennis champion/Martina Hingis

   _____

   _____

2. loud/rock band/The Who

   _____

   _____

3. noisy plane/Concorde

   _____

   _____

4. dry/desert/the Atacama Desert in Chile

   _____

   _____

5. fast/animal/the cheetah

   _____

   _____

Reading

5a Read the book review and complete the chart below.

One of my favorite books is _Brazzaville Beach_. It's by William Boyd, a British writer, and he wrote it in 1990. It's a thriller, but it's also a love story. It is set in Africa in the second half of the 20th century. The main character is a woman called Hope Clearwater. She is studying chimpanzees, and she notices that they can be very violent . . . It's a very exciting and interesting book. Read it!

	Book review
Name of book	_Brazzaville Beach_
Name of writer	_William Boyd_
Nationality of writer	
Date of writing	
Type of book	
Location (set in . . .)	
Time of story	
Main character	
Main event(s)	
Adjectives to describe book	

b Read the book review again. Write the order of the information.

_____ the opinion of the writer

_____ information about the writer of the book

_____ information about the characters

_____ a few details about the story

__1__ the name of the book

_____ the location and time of the story

_____ the type of book

Writing

6a Complete the chart with information about a book you like.

	Book you like
Name of book	
Name of writer	
Nationality of writer	
Date of writing	
Type of book	
Location (set in . . .)	
Time of story	
Main character	
Main event(s)	
Adjectives to describe book	

b Write a short review of your favorite book. Use Exercise 5 and the movie review on page 91 of your Student Book to help you.

Ex: One of my favorite books is . . .

_____

_____

_____

_____

_____

_____

_____

_____

_____

_____

Communication

1a Read about the events in St. Petersburg. Who is the website for? _____

Welcome to the St. Petersburg English Language Tourist Website. This week we have a number of cultural events and exhibitions taking place in the city. At the Hermitage Museum, there is an exhibition of impressionist paintings including Cézanne and Monet. At the Smolny Institute, there is an exhibition of abstract art, including paintings by Malevich. If you prefer sculpture, there is an exhibition of modern Russian sculpture at the Russian Museum.

For ballet lovers, the Kirov Ballet is performing *Swan Lake* at the Mariinsky Theater this week. You can buy tickets at the theater box office, which is open from 11:00 A.M. to 7:00 P.M. every day. If you prefer the opera, there is a performance of *The Marriage of Figaro* at the Mussorgsky Opera and Ballet Theater on Wednesday. You can buy tickets at the box office.

b Match the places to the exhibitions.

_____ 1. Mussorgsky Theater
_____ 2. Smolny Institute
_____ 3. Hermitage Museum
_____ 4. Mariinsky Theater
_____ 5. Russian Museum

a. modern Russian sculpture
b. impressionist paintings
c. *The Marriage of Figaro*
d. *Swan Lake*
e. abstract art

c Read the website again. Answer the questions.

Ex: Where can you see paintings by Monet?
   at the Hermitage Museum

1. Where can you see paintings by Malevich?
_____

2. What can you buy at the Mariinsky Theater box office?
_____

3. What time does the Mariinsky Theater box office open?
_____

4. When is the performance of *The Marriage of Figaro*?
_____

Grammar

2 Check (✓) the words that complete the sentences.

Ex: I like _____ better than tea.
   _____ **a.** drink coffee
   ✓ **b.** coffee
   _____ **c.** of coffee

1. I like novels, but my brother likes _____ newspapers.
   _____ **a.** read
   _____ **b.** reading
   _____ **c.** reads

2. Samuel likes cars _____ motorcycles.
   _____ **a.** of
   _____ **b.** better than
   _____ **c.** to

3. Does he _____ better than playing tennis?
   _____ **a.** likes swimming
   _____ **b.** like swims
   _____ **c.** like swimming

4. I like _____.
   _____ **a.** read than write
   _____ **b.** reading better than writing
   _____ **c.** reading than writing

3 Check (✓) the sentence (a or b) with the same meaning as the first sentence.

1. Jane is a good friend. Julie is my best friend.
   _____ **a.** I like Julie better than Jane.
   _____ **b.** I like Jane better than Julie.
2. We think art is more interesting than music.
   _____ **a.** We like art better than music.
   _____ **b.** We like music better than art.
3. Do you enjoy beef more than chicken?
   _____ **a.** Do you like chicken better than beef?
   _____ **b.** Do you like beef better than chicken?

4 Rewrite the sentences using *like* and *better than*.

Ex: She thinks drinking water is better than drinking fruit juice.
   She likes drinking water better than
   drinking fruit juice.

1. Dario buys more traditional art than modern art.
   _____
   _____
2. The children are more interested in playing than in reading.
   _____
   _____
3. I think action/adventure movies are more exciting than horror movies.
   _____
   _____
4. Blair watches television more than she listens to music.
   _____
   _____
5. We hardly ever visit museums, but we often go to concerts.
   _____
   _____
6. I like Italian food, but my favorite food is French.
   _____
   _____

5 Write responses. Use *will* + verbs in the box and the words in parentheses.

look at	check	call	get
~~answer~~	open	ask	go

Ex: There's someone at the door. (it)
   I'll answer it.

1. Where is the post office? (the map)
   _____
2. Can we meet at seven o'clock? (my schedule)
   _____
3. I can't open the door. (the key)
   _____
4. Does your husband want to come? (him)
   _____
5. She's very sick. (the doctor)
   _____
6. It's very hot in here. (the window)
   _____
7. We need some milk. (to the supermarket)
   _____

6 Correct the mistakes in the offers (1–3). Then match them to the pictures (B–D).

Ex: I'll to read the instructions.
   A   I'll read the instructions.

_____ **1.** I get it for you.
   _____
_____ **2.** I will gave you a refund.
   _____
_____ **3.** I'll turning on the lights.
   _____

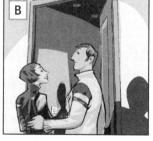

Grammar
Possessive pronouns; *one*/*ones*

1 Sometimes it is better to use a pronoun than a noun or noun phrase. <u>Underline</u> and replace the nouns (phrases) with pronouns.

> Ex: I love apples, especially red <u>apples</u>.
> _ones_____
>
> This is your coffee, and this is <u>my coffee</u>.
> _mine_____

1. The party isn't at my parents' house; it's at our house. _____
2. This isn't your pen; it's my pen. _____
3. Those flowers are lovely, especially the pink flowers. _____
4. A: Is this their house? B: No, the one with the blue door is their house. _____

Simple past: irregular verbs

2 Complete the sentences with the correct form of the verbs in the box.

> buy   have   not keep   leave   spend

1. We _____ a lot of money on clothes last weekend.
2. Penny _____ work at 5:00 yesterday.
3. We _____ pizza for dinner yesterday.
4. Allie and Jake _____ a new car last week.
5. A: Do you have the receipt? B: No, sorry. I _____ it.

Adverbs of frequency

3 Replace the <u>underlined</u> phrase with an adverb of frequency. Rewrite the sentence.

> Ex: I see my niece about <u>four times a year</u>.
> _I see my niece sometimes._____

1. I get up early <u>every day</u>. _____
2. We go to the movies on Friday evenings <u>almost every week</u>. _____

3. I watch soccer <u>about once a year.</u> _____
_____
4. I <u>don't</u> drink coffee after 6:00 in the evening.
_____
_____

Present continuous

4 Write sentences in the present continuous using the cues.

> Ex: What/Jean/wear/today?
> _What is Jean wearing today?_____

1. Dan and Donna/make/a Chinese meal
_____
_____
2. What/Steve/do/in the backyard?
_____
_____
3. Laura/wear/a long skirt/this evening
_____
_____
4. I/not/have/anything to eat
_____
_____

Simple present and continuous

5 Circle the correct form.

> ● ● ●
>
> Hi Emily,
>
> How are you? I *send*/*am sending* this email to ask if you are busy this afternoon. If not, can you come to my apartment for coffee? As you know, Gerry and I *usually work*/*are usually working* (**1.**) during the day, and we *don't get home*/*aren't getting home* (**2.**) before six in the evening. But today I *have*/*am having* (**3.**) a day at home. I *wait*/*am waiting* (**4.**) for a new stove. We bought it on Saturday, and it *comes*/*is coming* (**5.**) today—I hope! The store *brings*/*is bringing* (**6.**) it some time today, but I don't know when exactly. Our old stove broke last week, and we need a new one because we both *enjoy*/*are enjoying* (**7.**) cooking. Gerry and I *cook*/*are cooking* (**8.**) every evening, so it's very difficult without a stove. So *do you do*/*are you doing* (**9.**) anything today?
>
> Love,
> Karen

Adverbs of manner

6 Complete the sentences with adverbs of manner.

> Ex: That was careless. → You did that
> _carelessly_ .

1. Sue's a fast driver. → She drives
   _____ .

2. Kevin is a slow worker. → He works
   _____ .

3. That was a good match. → You played
   _____ .

4. It was an easy exercise. → We did it
   _____ .

5. She's a very quiet speaker. → She speaks very
   _____ .

6. Is that sofa comfortable? → Are you sitting
   _____ .

7. He's very careful when he chooses clothes. →
   He chooses clothes _____ .

Comparatives; superlatives

7 Write sentences using comparative and superlative adjectives and the information below.

	Age	Height	Weight
Joe	33	5'9"	180 lbs
Min	26	6'0"	165 lbs
Marc	40	6'2"	190 lbs

> Ex: Joe/Min—short _Joe is shorter than Min._
> Joe/Min/Marc—old _Marc is the oldest._

1. Min/Marc—heavy _____
   _____

2. Joe/Marc—old _____
   _____

3. Joe/Min/Marc—tall _____
4. Joe/Marc—short _____
   _____

5. Joe/Min/Marc—young _____
6. Joe/Min—heavy _____
   _____

7. Joe/Min/Marc—short _____
8. Min/Marc—young _____
   _____

9. Joe/Min—old _____
   _____

10. Joe/Min/Marc—heavy _____

Like + noun/gerund

8 Check (✓) the three sentences with no mistakes and correct the others.

_____ 1. We like old films than modern films.
   _____

_____ 2. I like white wine better than red wine.
   _____

_____ 3. Matt likes play football better than play badminton. _____
   _____

_____ 4. We're liking fish better than meat.
   _____

_____ 5. She likes opera better than ballet.
   _____

_____ 6. Do you like swim better than sunbathe?
   _____

_____ 7. Kate likes cycling to work better than taking the bus. _____
   _____

Vocabulary

9a Underline the word that does not belong.

> Ex: foggy   windy   _pretty_

1. thriller   ballet   animated movie
2. tight   sneakers   pants
3. novel   sweater   poetry
4. first   sixteenth   slim
5. comedy   impressionist   abstract
6. suit   hat   hot
7. belt   expensive   cheap

b Complete the sentences with the underlined words from Exercise 9a.

1. I need to wear a(n) _____ because my pants are loose.
2. It's always _____ in the summer.
3. Alison is very _____ now—she lost a lot of weight last year.
4. I don't like dancing, so I don't like
   _____ .
5. Put your _____ on—it's very cold.
6. Everyone likes _____ movies when they feel sad because they laugh and feel better.
7. This skirt is _____—can I have a bigger size, please?
8. Cathy is friendly and very _____ .

UNIT 10
Entertainment

Vocabulary

1a Underline the word that does not belong.

1. garage   drive   car   train
2. train   flight   station   platform
3. cycling   hiking   park   bungee jumping
4. commuting   rush hour   flight   traffic
5. passenger   ticket   plane   bicycle

b Use words from Exercise 1a to complete the sentences.

1. The train leaves from _____ 6.
2. It is always difficult to _____ a car in the middle of big cities.
3. _____ is usually from 5 P.M. to 6 P.M.
4. My parents gave me a(n) _____ for my tenth birthday.
5. I have a car, so I need a house with a(n) _____.

Grammar

2 Complete the interview with the words in the box. You will use some words more than once.

been	have	never	've
ever	haven't	went	

Interviewer: So, Della. Tell us about your travel experiences.

Della: Well, I _'ve_____ been to many different places around the world.

Interviewer: Where exactly have you _____ (1.)?

Della: I've been to New York and Washington. And I _____ (2.) to Rio de Janeiro last winter.

Interviewer: What about Asia? _____ (3.) you been to Bangkok?

Della: No, I've _____ (4.) been there. But I've been to Singapore.

Interviewer: What about Sydney?

Della: No. I _____ (5.) been there.

Interviewer: That's all very interesting, but have you _____ (6.) been to any resorts?

Della: Yes, I've been to The Sands in Mazatlán, Mexico. And I've been to Panarama in Vancouver, Canada.

Interviewer: When did you go there?

Della: Well, I went to Canada when I was a student. And I _____ (7.) to Mexico last summer.

Interviewer: Was that an all-inclusive resort?

Della: Yes, it was.

Interviewer: Have you _____ (8.) on any adventure vacations?

Della: No, I _____ (9.).

Interviewer: So, why do you want to be a vacation rep?

Della: Well, there was a vacation rep at the resort in Mexico. She was really good. That's the reason I applied for this job!

3 Read the questions and write short answers for Della. Then write true answers for yourself.

1. Have you ever been on an all-inclusive vacation?
   Della: _____
   You: _____
2. Have you ever been to a resort?
   Della: _____
   You: _____
3. Have you ever been on an adventure vacation?
   Della: _____
   You: _____

4 Look at the cues and write positive (✓) sentences, negative (✗) sentences, or questions (?) using the present perfect.

> **Ex:** We/to Canada (✓)
> _We've been to Canada._
>
> I/horseback riding (✗)
> _I haven't been horseback riding._
>
> You/on a long flight (?)
> _Have you been on a long flight?_

1. I/bungee jumping (✓)

   _____

2. We/to Bangkok (✗)

   _____

3. you/to London (?)

   _____

4. they/on an all-inclusive vacation (?)

   _____

5. John and Julie/to Australia (✗)

   _____

6. I/on an adventure vacation (✗)

   _____

7. Our parents/to Florida (✓)

   _____

8. you/to an IMAX theater (?)

   _____

9. We/hiking in the mountains (✓)

   _____

10. your cousins/to your new house (?)

    _____

5 Match the phrases to form sentences.

_____ 1.	Have you ever been	a. go there last year?
_____ 2.	Yes, they went there	b. there twice.
_____ 3.	Yes, I've been	c. I haven't.
_____ 4.	No,	d. to Seoul?
_____ 5.	Yes,	e. been there.
_____ 6.	Did you	f. in 2004.
_____ 7.	No, I haven't	g. I have.

6 Look at the pictures. Write questions with _Have you ever._ Then write true answers about you.

Have you ever been to a circus?
No, I haven't. or _Yes, I have._
I went last year.

_____
_____
_____

_____
_____
_____

_____
_____
_____

_____
_____
_____

_____
_____
_____

Vocabulary

1   Match the postcard excerpts with the types of activities in the box.

> cultural activities   water sports
> winter sport   sightseeing

1 │ Jason has tried sailing and windsurfing and . . . _____

2 │ We've visited all the museums and have been to the famous ballet. _____

3 │ I'm really tired. I've walked for hours in the city today. _____

4 │ Serena has spent every day skiing. _____

Reading

2a   Read the ads. What types of activities do they describe? Use the activities from Exercise 1.

b   Which vacation is the best for these people? Write the places.

1. My friends and I want to go on vacation in the summer. We're all 18 or 19 and we like the sun. We want to have a good time! _____

2. Stephen and I want to get away for a few nights. We don't like the sun, and we don't want to be active. We belong to a classical music club. _____

3. My girlfriend wants to go on vacation during the winter, but we're not sure what kind of vacation. We don't want to stay in a city, but a beach in the winter isn't a good idea. We don't ski, so that's a problem. _____

3   In which place(s) can you do these things?
> Ex: stay in a downtown hotel   _Verona_

1. travel to the place by road _____
2. take lessons _____
3. enjoy a busy nightlife _____
4. stay in an apartment _____
5. go swimming _____

1 ___winter sports___

Beaver Creek

One of Colorado's best-known resorts, high in the Rockies, Beaver Creek offers something for skiers of all ages and levels, even for non-skiers.

You can stay in the main hotel or in an apartment, where you can cook your own meals or have your meals in one of the first-class restaurants at the resort.

For experienced skiers there are runs of all levels of difficulty. If this is your first time skiing, or if you haven't skied for a long time, there are classes at all levels.

2 _____

BARBADOS'S HOTTEST RESORT

Crystal Cove is one of Barbados's busiest and most popular resorts, with many sandy beaches for swimming, sailing, windsurfing, and sunbathing. It also has the best nightlife on the island with many restaurants plus nightclubs for all ages. Our fabulous four-star hotel has everything you need: two restaurants, a health club and gym, two swimming pools, a private beach, stores, and a spa.

3 _____

Verona opera season

Short breaks for opera lovers

Plan your own short vacation in one of Italy's most romantic cities. Travel by air or road and stay in a three-star downtown hotel for two, three, or four nights. The price includes:

- travel to Verona
- bed and breakfast
- two tickets to the opera
- two tickets to the ballet

Grammar

4a Write about people on vacation from the ads in Exercise 2a. Use the words in parentheses and write a positive (✓) or a negative (✗) sentence.

> **Ex:** Aimi is on vacation in Colorado.
>
> (go to the beach) (✗) _Aimi hasn't been to_
> _the beach._
>
> (learn to ski) (✓) _She's learned to ski._

1. (cook all her meals) (✗)

   _____

2. (visit the sights) (✓)

   _____

Paul is on vacation in Verona.

3. (see an opera) (✓)

   _____

4. (learn to ski) (✗)

   _____

5. (go on a city tour) (✓)

   _____

Karl and Tara are on vacation in Barbados.

6. (have a quiet week) (✗)

   _____

7. (go to many nightclubs) (✓)

   _____

8. (spend hours on the beach) (✓)

   _____

b Complete the chart.

	Base verb	Past participle
1.	become	_____
2.	catch	_____
3.	drive	_____
4.	forget	_____
5.	keep	_____
6.	meet	_____
7.	ride	_____
8.	wear	_____

c Complete the sentences with the present perfect. Use the verbs in the chart in Exercise 4b.

1. _____ you ever _____ a horse?
2. Oh no! I _____ my key!
3. I _____ never _____ these pants.
4. _____ you _____ my friend Aileen?
5. Gerald _____ an enormous fish.
6. Your son _____ very tall now he's older.
7. My brother _____ a fancy sports car.
8. _____ your parents _____ photos of you when you were a child?

Writing

5a Choose one of the places in Exercise 2a to go to on vacation. Read the questions and take notes.

1. Where are you staying? (hotel/apartment)

   _____

2. What is it like?

   _____

3. What is the resort like?

   _____

4. What has the weather been like?

   _____

5. Who are you with?

   _____

6. What have you done? What has your friend (wife, etc.) done?

   _____

b Write a postcard to a friend. Use your notes and the Writing Bank on page 133 of your Student Book.

_____

_____

_____

_____

_____

_____

_____

_____

_____

_____

Reading

Technology_review_

Citybug electric scooter

Star rating ★★★☆☆

Commuting in big cities is getting more and more <u>difficult</u>. You can't park cars. Buses are slow. Trains are expensive and crowded. What can you do?

Cycling is the answer for many people. It's <u>great</u> if your city streets are flat and you are fit and have a lot of energy. But many people get tired, and it's very difficult to ride up <u>hills</u>.

So, if you want to find an easy way to commute and you don't have a lot of energy, try the Citybug electric <u>scooter</u>.

The Citybug has an electric engine with a <u>top speed</u> of 14 miles per hour (22 kilometers per hour). It loves going up hills!

Because the Citybug is electric, you don't need to go to the <u>gas station</u>! You just <u>connect</u> the Citybug to the electricity in your house for one or two hours. So it's very cheap.

Riding the Citybug is easy, but the seat and the wheels are small, so it isn't very comfortable. Of course it isn't fast, and it weighs 46 pounds (21 kg) so it's pretty heavy. But it's easy to park, and you don't need a driver's license, so adults or children can use it.

[Check] our price comparison page for the latest prices.

Search [   ] Products ‹› [GO]

1a Look at the article. Check (✓) where it is from.

_____ **A.** a newspaper

_____ **B.** a magazine

_____ **C.** an Internet page

b Read the article. Match the <u>underlined</u> words to these descriptions.

Ex: small mountains _hills_

1. a place where you can buy gas for your car

   _____

2. the fastest speed _____

3. not easy _____

4. look at _____

5. small motorcycle _____

6. join two things together _____

7. very good _____

c Write notes in the chart.

The Citybug electric scooter	
Advantages	Disadvantages
You don't need a lot of energy.	_It isn't very fast._

Vocabulary

2 Match the words to make phrases.

_____	1. one-way	a.	hour
_____	2. long	b.	class
_____	3. economy	c.	date
_____	4. high-speed	d.	agent
_____	5. rush	e.	train
_____	6. departure	f.	ticket
_____	7. travel	g.	flight

3 Use phrases from Exercise 2 to complete the sentences.

1. I go to work on a(n) _____ because it's fast and efficient.

2. Tuesday October 15th. Is that your _____ ?

3. I don't want to come back, so I need a(n) _____ .

4. Sometimes the seats in _____ on a flight are very small and uncomfortable.

5. In New York the morning _____ is between 7:00 and 9:00 A.M.

Grammar

4 Write sentences with the cues. Use the *-ing* form and adjectives in the box.

> scary   relaxing   expensive   dangerous
> ~~easy~~   difficult   healthy   exciting

Ex: send/text messages
   Sending text messages is easy.

1. watch/horror movies

   _____

2. eat/a lot of fruit and vegetables

   _____

3. drive/in fog

   _____

4. learn/a foreign language

   _____

5. swim/in warm water

   _____

6. visit/new places

   _____

7. fly/in business class

   _____

5 Rewrite the sentences using the *-ing* form.
   Ex: It's cheap to travel by subway in Paris.
   Traveling by subway is cheap in Paris.

1. It's difficult to park a car in big cities.

   _____

2. It's easy to get information from the Internet.

   _____

3. It's romantic to send flowers to your wife or girlfriend. _____

   _____

4. It's nice to get an email from your best friend.

   _____

5. It's interesting to watch the news on TV.

   _____

Communication

6 Complete the conversation with the sentences in the box.

> How much is that flight?
> Is it a direct flight?
> Economy class, please.
> ~~Saturday, August 21.~~
> What time does it leave?
> Round-trip. We'd like to come
>   back on Saturday, August 28.

Stephen: Do you sell airline tickets to Brazil? We'd like two tickets from Chicago to Rio de Janeiro.

Travel agent: OK. What is your departure date?

Stephen: 1. *Saturday, August 21* _____ .

Travel agent: One way or round-trip?

Stephen: 2. _____

Travel agent: Business class or economy class?

Stephen: 3. _____

Travel agent: Let me see . . . We have a flight with United Airlines.

Stephen: 4. _____

Travel agent: It's $650.

Stephen: 5. _____

Travel agent: No, it stops in Houston.

Stephen: 6. _____

Travel agent: It leaves Chicago at 10:30 in the morning.

Reading

1a Read the guidelines at the right and choose the best answer.

The notice gives _____

A. information and advice

B. information and rules

C. advice

D. rules

b Match the underlined words in the guidelines to the pictures.

1 _____   3 _____

2 _____   4 _____

c Match the words to their meanings.

_____ **1.** proof

_____ **2.** carry-on luggage

_____ **3.** checked luggage

_____ **4.** boarding

a. The bags you give at the check-in desk.

b. Entering a plane.

c. This shows that something is true.

d. Small bags you take on the plane.

SUNSHINE VACATIONS

If you are flying with *Go Faster Airlines*, please read these guidelines before you go to the airport.

Documents

Go Faster Airlines uses an electronic check-in system. You don't have to bring your tickets to the check-in desk, but you have to bring proof of your identity (including your photo): for example, a passport, driver's license, or identity card.
If you are flying to another country, you have to show your passport.

Luggage

With *Go Faster Airlines* you can check a maximum of 44 pounds of luggage. You can take a maximum of 11 pounds of carry-on luggage. You can't put sharp objects in your carry-on luggage. You have to put them in your checked luggage. Your suitcase has to have a label with your name and address. The label doesn't have to have your flight number because that is on the electronic label.

Electronic devices

You have to switch off all electronic devices before boarding the plane. You can't use your cell phone inside the plane.

Grammar

2 Read the guidelines in Exercise 1 again. Check (✓) the correct columns in the chart.

	Necessary	Not necessary	Possible	Not possible
1. bring tickets to the check-in desk				
2. bring proof of your identity				
3. show your passport when you fly to another country				
4. check 44 pounds of luggage				
5. take more than 11 pounds of carry-on luggage				
6. put sharp objects in your carry-on luggage				
7. put a label on your suitcase with your name and address				
8. put your flight number on your suitcase label				
9. switch off electronic devices before you board the plane				
10. use a cell phone inside the plane				

3 Use these airport rules to write two sentences with *can't* and three sentences with *have to*.

> ### Rules
> - Be at check-in two hours before your departure time.
> - ~~No smoking on the plane.~~
> - Don't take drinks onto the plane.
> - Turn off your cell phone before you board the plane.
> - Don't take food on the plane.
> - Wear your seat belt during the flight.

can't

Ex: *You can't smoke on the plane.*

1. _____

2. _____

have to

3. _____

4. _____

5. _____

4 Complete the sentences using a form of *have to, don't have to, can,* or *can't*.

Ex: It isn't necessary to wear a suit in my office.
I *don't have to wear a suit in my office.*

In New York, people aren't allowed to smoke in restaurants.
You *can't smoke in restaurants in New York.*

1. It isn't possible to drive a car when you are only 13 years old.
You _____ .

2. Bring a friend to the party if you want to.
I _____ .

3. In my office it isn't possible to use our cell phones.
We _____ .

4. Show your receipt to the manager.
You _____ .

5. There's no parking near the theater.
You _____ .

6. It isn't necessary for Amanda to pay because she's a member of the club.
Amanda _____ .

7. We accept payment by cash or credit card.
You _____ .

8. It isn't necessary for David and Lucy to get visas to go to Canada.
David and Lucy _____ .

Vocabulary

5 Complete the sentences with the words in the box.

> | | | |
> |---|---|---|
> | fine | turn right | driver's license |
> | obey | seat belt | traffic lights |
> | offense | driving test | |

1. There are three colors on _____: red, yellow, and green.

2. It is a(n) _____ to go faster than the speed limit.

3. In most countries drivers have to wear a(n) _____ .

4. I'm a good driver. I don't have any points on my _____ .

5. Did you pass your _____?

6. I paid a $75 _____ because I drove faster than the speed limit.

7. Do you always _____ traffic laws?

8. In most places in the US, you can _____ on a red light.

Communication

1 Read the interviews on the right. Write the number of the interview by the person.

_____ an American woman

_____ an older English man, he didn't like school

_____ a teacher of French and Spanish

2a Check (✓) the interview that has the answer.

Which person or people . . .	1	2	3
1. liked math and geography?	____	____	____
2. left school early?	____	____	____
3. didn't go to college?	____	____	____
4. enjoyed languages at school?	____	____	____
5. got married in Colombia?	____	____	____

b Complete the chart for interviews 2 and 3.

	1	2	3
1. Age started school?	5		
2. Location of school?	London		
3. Time spent at school?	9 years		
4. Enjoyed school?	no		
5. Favorite subject(s)?	PE		
6. Went to college?	no		

1
A: Excuse me, can I ask you some questions about your schooldays?
B: You can, but it was a long time ago!
A: When did you start school?
B: When I was about five, I think. Yes, I was five.
A: And where did you go to school?
B: In London. I was there through all my years at school.
A: How long did you stay at school?
B: Oh, only about nine years, I think. Yes, I left school when I was 14.
A: Did you enjoy school?
B: No, I hated it.
A: What was your favorite subject?
B: I didn't have one . . . well, I suppose it was PE.
A: Did you go to college?
B: Oh, no. I left school and I went to work. I wanted to make some money.

2
A: Excuse me, can I ask you some questions about your schooldays?
B: Yes, sure.
A: When did you start school?
B: When I was six.
A: And where did you go to school?
B: In Texas. I'm from the US, so I went to school there.
A: How long did you stay in school?
B: From six to eighteen, so, what's that? Twelve years.
A: Did you enjoy school?
B: Yeah, it was OK.
A: What was your favorite subject?
B: I liked math and geography.
A: Did you go to college?
B: Well, I started college—I started studying math, but it was difficult, so I left. Then I traveled to Colombia, and I met my husband, and, well, that's it.

3
A: Excuse me, can I ask you some questions about your schooldays?
B: Yes, of course.
A: When did you start school?
B: Oh, the usual age, five, I think.
A: And where did you go to school?
B: In Canada.
A: How long did you stay at school?
B: Er, until I was 18, so about 13 years in total.
A: Did you enjoy school?
B: Yes, I did. I really liked it.
A: What was your favorite subject?
B: I loved languages—French and Spanish.
A: Did you go to college?
B: Yes, I finished college two years ago—I studied French and Spanish there, too, and now I'm teaching French and Spanish, and I really enjoy it!

Grammar

3 Write the questions that the interviewer asked. Use the cues in the chart in Exercise 2b to help you. (Not all the questions need a *wh-* word.)

Ex: _When did you start school?_

1. _____
2. _____
3. _____
4. _____
5. _____

4a Complete the groups of questions with the *wh-* words in the box.

how many	how	what	when
where	who	~~which~~	why

Ex: _Which_____ subjects did you take?/ school did you go to?/class do you like best?

1. _____ students are in your class?/ languages can you speak?/subjects do you have on Monday?

2. _____ do you sit next to?/is your favorite teacher?/do you live with?

3. _____ is the school?/is your house?/do you go in the evenings?

4. _____ time is it?/do you do on the weekend?/did you watch on TV yesterday?

5. _____ do you get to the school?/ do you spend your free time?/did you find this school?

6. _____ do you get up?/did you start learning English?/do you exercise?

7. _____ are you learning English?/do you live in the city?/did you say that?

b Write a question from Exercise 4a for each answer.

1. _Where do you go in the evenings?_____
   We often go to a café or to the movies.

2. _____
   Two years ago.

3. _____
   My parents and my younger brother.

4. _____
   I take the bus.

5. _____
   I went to Kingston High School.

6. _____
   A program about the Sahara desert.

7. _____
   Because I need it for my job.

8. _____
   Physics, math, and English.

c Answer the questions in Exercise 4b with true answers for you.

1. _____
2. _____
3. _____
4. _____
5. _____
6. _____
7. _____
8. _____

Writing

5a Read these questions about learning English in your country. Take notes.

1. When do children start learning English?
   _____

2. Is English the first or second foreign language?
   _____

3. Is it a compulsory or optional subject?
   _____

4. How many years do they study English?
   _____

5. Which parts of the language are most important at school (grammar, reading . . .)?
   _____

6. Where do people study English when they leave school?
   _____

7. Why do people usually study English after they finish school?
   _____

b Write a short description of English studies in your country. _____
_____
_____
_____
_____

Grammar

1a Cristina graduated two weeks ago, and she's very busy. Look at her schedule for this week and answer the questions with complete sentences.

Monday July 12th	Thursday July 15th
travel to Chicago A.M. (Regent Hotel)	bank manager 2:00 P.M.
prepare for interview P.M.	
Tuesday July 13th	**Friday July 16th**
interview for job 9:30 A.M.	swimming with David 9.00 A.M.
train back home 1:00 P.M.	driving test 4.30 P.M.
Wednesday July 14th	**Saturday July 17th**
start summer school 10:00 A.M.	shopping with Marta 11.30 A.M.
	Bailey's nightclub 10:00 P.M. with Javier
	Sunday July 18th lunch with Mom and Dad 1:30 P.M.

Ex: Is Cristina traveling to Chicago on Monday?
Yes, she's traveling to Chicago on Monday morning.

Is she interviewing for housing on Tuesday?
No, she's interviewing for a job on Tuesday.

1. Is she catching the train home on Tuesday morning?

_____

2. Is she starting a job on Wednesday?

_____
_____

3. Is she seeing the bank manager on Thursday?

_____

4. Is she taking her driving test on Friday morning?

_____

5. Is she going to the movies with Javier on Saturday?

_____
_____

6. Is she going to her mom and dad's on Sunday?

_____
_____

b Write questions about Cristina using the cues. Then write short answers.

Ex: stay/at the Regent Hotel/in Chicago
Is Cristina staying at the Regent Hotel in Chicago?
Yes, she is.

What/do/on Monday afternoon
What is she doing on Monday afternoon?
Preparing for the job interview.

1. interview/on Tuesday morning

_____
_____
_____

2. What time/catch/the train/on Tuesday

_____
_____
_____

3. When/meet/the bank manager

_____
_____
_____

4. go swimming/with David/Friday

_____
_____
_____

5. go shopping/on Saturday afternoon

_____
_____
_____

6. Who/Cristina/go shopping/with

_____
_____
_____

Vocabulary

2a Complete the chart with the words in the box.

> biology   professor   university
> college   instructor   ~~high school~~
> English   doctorate
> physics   bachelor's degree

Educational institutions	Qualifications	People teaching	School subjects
high school			

b Add at least one more word in each column.

3 Circle the correct adjective.

1. In my school we have to take one foreign language, but the second one is *compulsory/ optional.*

2. I can't afford to stop working, so I'm going to school *full-time/part-time* two evenings a week.

3. My parents sent me to a *private/public* school because we didn't have a lot of money.

4. I enjoy studying at home on my own, so a *classroom-learning/distance-learning* course is very good for me.

5. When I graduate college I will earn a *bachelor's degree/driver's license.*

6. I like learning about plants and animals, my favorite subject is *physics/biology.*

4 Complete the chart with the sentences.

> Let's say Tuesday evening at 7:00.
> ~~Can you come at four o'clock?~~
> I'm afraid we can't come then.
> How about early Tuesday instead?

How To:

Suggest a time	*Can you come at four o'clock?*
Refuse politely	
Suggest an alternative	
Make an appointment	

5 Complete the dialog with the sentences from Exercise 4.

A: Excuse me, can I make an appointment to see you about our son's schoolwork?

B: Of course. I'm free on Friday afternoon. *Can you come at four o'clock?* _____.

A: Oh, I'm sorry, _____
_____ (1.). My husband's working on Friday afternoon.

B: So, are evenings better?

A: Yes, they are.

B: OK, _____
_____ (2.)? I always stay late at school then.

A: Yes, that's fine.

B: Good. _____
_____ (3.).

A: OK. Thank you.

Vocabulary

1 Complete the postcard with words and expressions in the box.

> tunnel   island   hiking
> coast   sailing   canyon
> white-water rafting

Dear Harry,

We're having a great vacation. Our hotel is near the
_____ (1.)—it's just a few hundred feet
to the ocean. There are many activities here. Last
Wednesday we went _____ (2.) on the
river. It was scary but very exciting! The river is at the
bottom of a huge _____ (3.).

On Friday we went to a small _____ (4.).
There was a nice beach, so we sunbathed in the morning.
In the afternoon we went _____ (5.) on a
beautiful old boat.

Tomorrow we're going _____ (6.) in the
hills.

Give my love to Mom and Dad.

Love,

Daniela

Grammar

2 Complete the conversation with the correct forms of *be going to*.

Linda: So, what are you going to do this summer?

Anthony: Well, I don't have my tickets yet, but I'm planning to go to Canada. I *'m going to* visit my cousins in Vancouver.

Linda: Really? That sounds exciting.

Anthony: Yes. I've never been to Canada.

Linda: People say it's beautiful. _____ you _____ (1.) travel around or stay in one place?

Anthony: Well, I think I _____ (2.) fly to Vancouver and stay with my cousins first. Then they _____ (3.) take me to Whistler in the mountains.

Linda: Mountain climbing?

Anthony: No, we _____ (4.) go hiking. We _____ (5.) spend three weeks hiking around the Rocky Mountains. Then I _____ (6.) drive down to the US border. I want to see Seattle.

Linda: _____ your girlfriend _____ (7.) travel with you?

Anthony: Well, she isn't a teacher like me, so she can only take two weeks of vacation. She _____ (8.) join me in Seattle. We _____ (9.) stay there for ten days, and then we're going to fly back together at the beginning of September.

Linda: You're lucky. It sounds wonderful!

3 Rewrite the sentences using *going to* and the expressions in parentheses.

> Ex: We stayed with our uncle last week. (visit our cousins/next month)
> *We're going to visit our cousins next month.*
>
> She didn't buy any pasta at the store. (not cook lasagna/this evening)
> *She isn't going to cook lasagna this evening.*

1. I started the course in June. (finish the course/September)

   _____

2. Did you write a letter to the travel agent? (no/I/send an email/tomorrow)

   _____

   _____

3. Last year they stayed with relatives in France. (this year/stay with friends/in Spain)

   _____

   _____

4. Henry went white-water rafting in Colorado last year. (sailing/in Canada/next year)

   _____

   _____

5. She didn't study physics in high school. (not study science/in college)

   _____

   _____

4 The people in the pictures are thinking about their intentions. Write a sentence about what they are thinking.

We're going to buy a dishwasher.

Reading

5a Read the conversation in Exercise 2 again. What is the connection between the photo and the map? _____

b Put Anthony's intentions in the correct order.

_____ go hiking in the Rocky Mountains

_____ stay in Seattle

_____ fly home

_____ drive to the US border

_____ stay with his cousins

_1_ fly to Vancouver

_____ go to Whistler

c Circle the correct choice.

1. Anthony is going to stay with his *girlfriend/ cousins* in Vancouver.

2. Anthony and his cousins are going to go *mountain climbing/hiking*.

3. He's going to *drive/fly* to Seattle.

4. Anthony's girlfriend *isn't/is* a teacher.

Vocabulary

6 Correct the mistakes in the underlined words.

Ex: I'm going to finish the course summer next.
    next summer

1. He's going to take his driving test this later year. _____

2. What are you going to do week next?
   _____

3. Is she going to visit him tommorrow?
   _____

4. We're going to take the children hiking the next week after. _____

5. Are you going to take a vacation year next?
   _____

Reading

1a Read the letter quickly and choose the correct answer. The letter is ____.

    a. a letter to a friend who is a web designer.

    b. a formal cover letter for a job as a web designer.

    c. an informal letter to a friend who lives abroad.

> **A**   Dear Richard,
>
> **B**   Things are fine here in Beijing. My job isn't very interesting but I have a lot of exciting plans. You know I want to be a web designer. Well, I'm going to start a part-time computing course to learn all about web design! It's at the local college, two evenings a week for three months. We're going to study a program called Dreamweaver. You can use it to make websites. Do you remember my friend Hung? Well, we have a great plan. One day we're going to start our own web design company! It's very exciting.
>
> **C**   Give my love to your parents. Please write again soon and tell me all about your new co-workers!
>
> **D**   Thanks for your last letter. Congratulations on your new job in Boston—it's a great place for a young architect! It was really interesting to hear all about your new office. I'm sorry you only get two weeks of vacation, but I know that's pretty normal in the US.
>
> **E**   Love,
>
>   Lijuan

b Put paragraphs B, C, and D in the correct order.   **1.** ___   **2.** ___   **3.** ___

2   Read the letter and write short answers.

    Ex: What does Richard have? _a new job_

    1. What is Richard's job? _____

    2. Where does Richard work? _____

    3. Why is Lijuan sorry? _____

    4. What is normal in the United States?

    _____

    5. Where does Lijuan live? _____

    6. Is Lijuan's job interesting? _____

    7. What is Lijuan's ambition? _____

    8. Why is she starting a part-time course?

    _____

    9. Why do people use Dreamweaver?

    _____

    10. What is Hung and Lijuan's plan?

    _____

Vocabulary

3a Complete the chart with the letters in the box. You can use each letter more than once.

    (n   g   r   i   o   e)

b Write these categories in the chart.

    People   Activities   Events

1. _____		2. _____		3. _____	
act . . .		sess . . .		produc . . .	
sing . . .	_i_ _ _	elect . . .	_ _ _	play . . .	_ _
danc . . .		competit . . .		perform . . .	

Grammar

4 Match the actions to the purposes. Then use the information to write sentences.

_e_ **1.** I'm going to start a part-time computing course

____ **2.** You can use a computer

____ **3.** She's joining a gym

____ **4.** Mike uses his bicycle

____ **5.** We went to Cartagena

____ **6.** I'm going on a diet

____ **7.** I'm going to improve my English

a. get fit

b. visit our grandparents

c. send emails

d. lose weight

e. ~~learn all about web design~~

f. get a better job

g. commute to work

1. _I'm going to start a part-time computing course to learn all about web design._

2. _____

3. _____

4. _____

5. _____

6. _____

7. _____

5 Put the words in the correct order to make sentences.

Ex: sunbathe/the beach/I/to/go to
I go to the beach to sunbathe.

1. Jane/to/her boyfriend/Quito/flew/to visit

_____

2. to play/My son/his computer/uses/games

_____

3. a stereo/to listen to/I'm/going/get/to/music

_____

4. We/food/to buy/to/the market/go/fresh

_____

5. to see/My brother/the new museum to/went

_____

Writing

6a Look at Exercise 1. Copy the sentences Lijuan uses to do the following things.

Ex: mention the last letter she received
Thanks for your last letter.

1. make a positive comment about Richard's job

_____

2. describe her feelings about Richard's vacation

_____

3. say something general about her life

_____

4. end her letter

_____

b In informal letters we often use contracted forms, modifiers, and adjectives. Find two more examples of each of these in Lijuan's letter.

1. contracted forms: _isn't_ _____ _____

2. modifiers: _very_ _____ _____

3. adjectives: _interesting_ _____ _____

7a You are going to write a letter to a close friend. Before you start, study this information.

Your friend	You
Her name is Isabel. She is Australian.	Last week you started a new job.
Last month she moved to a new house in Sydney.	You are going to start a yoga class at the gym next month.
She is going to visit you in your country next summer.	You are going to buy a new cell phone tomorrow.

b Now plan your letter to Isabel. Use these notes.

First paragraph
- Thank Isabel for her last letter.
- Describe your feelings about her news.

Second paragraph
- Tell Isabel about your new job.
- Describe your plans for the future.

Third paragraph
- Ask her to write soon and end the letter.

c Write the letter on a separate piece of paper.
- Write about 150 words and use your imagination.
- Use contracted forms, modifiers, and adjectives.
- Use Lijuan's letter as a model.
- Then check for grammar and spelling mistakes.

Communication

1a Read the conversation. Check (✓) the ambitions the friends talk about.

____ be an accountant   ____ go around the world

____ become a politician   ____ win a lot of money

____ be a rock singer   ____ be a businesswoman

Jay: What's wrong, Tina? You look bored today.

Tina: I am, well, I'm not bored right now, but I'm really bored with my job. It's the same thing every day. I really want to do something different.

Jay: Like what? Find another job?

Tina: Well, I don't know. I suppose I'd like to win a lot of money and retire!

Dee: Come on, Tina, I know you. You can't stand doing nothing. You love being busy.

Tina: Hmm, maybe . . . but you have to think about escaping sometimes.

Matt: Yes, that's right. I would like to travel around the world and see lots of interesting places.

Dee: Matt, you hate flying. You're not going to get on a long flight!

Matt: I hate flying, but I love going to new places. Anyway, don't you ever want to change your life, Dee?

Dee: Yes, of course. I'd like to become a politician and change the world.

Jay: I wouldn't like that. Everyone hates politicians. Anyway, you're a businesswoman, so you already have that kind of life.

Dee: I don't think so . . .

Jay: You know what I've always wanted to be?

Matt: What?

Jay: A rock singer.

Tina: Really? But you play the guitar.

Jay: I know, and I love playing the guitar. But I enjoy singing, too, and I'm taking singing lessons now.

Matt: I didn't know that.

Jay: And I've joined a new rock band—we play in nightclubs on the weekends, and people like us.

Dee: So what about your job?

Jay: My job as an accountant? I'm going to do it for another year or so, but the band is making a CD later this year, so . . .

Dee: Wow! You're going to be famous!

---

b Complete the sentences with the friends' ambitions.

1. Tina would like to _____.
2. Matt would like to _____.
3. Dee would like to _____.
4. Jay would like to _____.

Grammar

2 Read the conversation in Exercise 1a again and complete the summary.

Tina wants _to do_ something different. She'd like _____ (1.) a lot of money and retire, but she can't stand _____ (2.) all day.

Matt would like _____ (3.) around the world, but he hates _____ (4.).

Dee would like _____ (5.) a politician and change the world.

Jay wouldn't like _____ (6.) a politician because everyone hates them. He's always wanted _____ (7.) a rock singer—he loves _____ (8.) the guitar, and he enjoys _____ (9.).

3 What do the people want to do with their lives? Why? Look at the pictures. Then write sentences using words in the box.

> ~~work in the yard~~   be with children
> drive fast   help young people
> listen to music   visit different countries

1. *He would like to have a large yard because he enjoys working in the yard.*

2. _____

3. _____

4. _____

5. _____

6. _____

1 Large yard
2 Race car driver
3 Good stereo system
4 Teacher
5 Vacation rep
6 Lots of grandchildren

4a There are five more grammatical mistakes in Michelle's letter. <u>Underline</u> and number them.

As you know, I left my job last month. I worked in an office, and (1) <u>I really hated be</u> inside all the time. Now I have to find another job. I wouldn't like working in an office again, so I'm thinking about some more training. I really enjoy to swim and I would like to becoming a swimming instructor. But there's a problem. Part of the exam is written, and I can't stand to take written exams—I always do them very badly. I really want start teaching in the summer. Can you suggest ways to study for the exam?

b Correct the sentences from Exercise 4a.

1. *I really hated being inside*

2. _____

3. _____

4. _____

5. _____

6. _____

Writing

5a Take notes about your ambitions for the future in these four areas.

- work and study

  _____

- marriage and children

  _____

- travel and vacations

  _____

- sports / leisure activities

  _____

b Write a paragraph about your ambitions for the future. Say why you want to do these things. Use the example below to help you.

I really enjoy watching movies, so I would like to take a night course on film history. One day I'd like to work in film or TV. I'm happy with my boyfriend, but I don't want to have children because I don't really like being with young children—well, not at the moment anyway. I want to travel all around the world because I love seeing different places. I'd like to play sports all my life because I enjoy being active and keeping fit. I think I would also like to go on an adventure tour one day.

Grammar
Present perfect

1 Complete the questions and answers with *has, have, 's, 've, ever, been,* or *went.* Use contracted forms.

1. A: Have you _____ been to England?

   B: No, I _____ never been there.

2. A: _____ your father been on a long flight?

   B: Yes, he _____ to Singapore last winter.

3. A: _____ you ever been to a rock concert?

   B: Yes, I _____.

4. A: Has your wife ever _____ to Chile?

   B: Yes, she _____ been to Argentina and Chile.

5. A: _____ you been to a theme park?

   B: Yes, we _____ been many times.

2 Write present perfect questions (?) or negative sentences (✗) with the cues.

Ex: she/ever/see/an opera (?)

   Has she ever seen an opera?

   I/go to/a zoo (✗)

   I haven't been to a zoo.

1. I/spend/a lot of money (✗)

   _____

2. you/take/the driving test (?)

   _____

3. she/write/any postcards (?)

   _____

4. I/see/that movie (✗)

   _____

5. The students/do/their homework (✗)

   _____

6. you/ever/play/golf (?)

   _____

7. Lena/visit/her parents (?)

   _____

8. We/go/on vacation this year (✗)

   _____

9. Henry/buy/a newspaper today (✗)

   _____

10. you/have/lunch (?)

    _____

Gerund as subject

3 Check (✓) the correct sentences. Underline and correct the mistakes.

Ex: _✓_ I think waiting for a bus is boring.

   _____ Cycle is popular in Amsterdam.
   Cycling

_____ 1. Today fly is very popular. _____

_____ 2. In New York going to the movies is expensive. _____

_____ 3. Swimming is very relaxing. _____

_____ 4. On the Internet, pay by credit card is easy. _____

_____ 5. Sunbathing are bad for you. _____

Can/can't, have to/don't have to

4 Look at the flier. Then rewrite the numbered sentences using *can, can't, have to,* or *don't have to.*

Information for Brindsley College Students

   • Don't park in the teachers' parking lot
1. • Don't smoke in the buildings.
2.   (Smoking is OK outside.)
3. • Don't bring food or drinks into the classrooms.
4.   (It is possible to get coffee and tea in the café.)
5. • Show an identity card when you arrive on campus.
6. • Don't use cell phones during class.
7. • Using the computers in the library is possible in the evenings.
8.   (It isn't necessary to pay to use the computers)
9. • Bring a pen and some paper to class.
10.   (But it isn't necessary to bring a dictionary.)

Ex: Don't park in the teachers' parking lot.

   Students . . .

   can't park in the teachers' parking lot.

1. _____
2. _____
3. _____
4. _____
5. _____
6. _____
7. _____
8. _____
9. _____
10. _____

Present continuous for future

5 Complete the conversations using the words in parentheses and the present continuous.

Ex: Q: _Is Steve arriving_ tomorrow? (Steve arrive)

A: No. He_'s arriving_ on Sunday. (arrive)

1. Q: What _____ on the weekend? (you do)

   A: We _____ the children to the beach. (take)

2. Q: _____ here on the bus? (Jane come)

   A: No. She _____ here. (drive)

3. Q: When _____? (your friends leave)

   A: They _____ on Saturday. (go)

4. Q: What _____ this evening? (you cook)

   A: I _____, I'm going to a restaurant. (not cook)

be going to

6 Complete the letter with the words in parentheses and the correct form of *be going to*.

Dear Hilary,

Thanks for your last letter. Congratulations on your new job! Things are very busy for us at the moment. We moved into our new house last week. It's very old, and there are a lot of things we want to do! We _____ (**1.** build) a new kitchen because the old one is really small. My brother-in-law _____ (**2.** do) the work because he's a builder. We _____ (**3.** not buy) the equipment from the local stores—they are very expensive! Amanda _____ (**4.** buy) all the equipment from the Internet! I think she _____ (**5.** get) one of those huge refrigerators! We both love cooking so we _____ (**6.** have) a really good stove, but Amanda _____ (**7.** not get) a microwave because she hates microwaved food! We also want to do things in the yard. I _____ (**8.** buy) a lot of beautiful new plants.

How are things with you? What's your new job like? _____ (**9.** you stay) there for a long time? Write to me and let me know your plans. _____ (**10.** you/visit) us soon?

Love,
Erik

Verb + infinitive/gerund

7 Circle the correct choice.

1. Yoko hates _sunbathing/sunbathe,_ so she doesn't like _going/go_ to the beach.
2. I _like/'d like_ to go to China next summer.
3. Felix loves _play/playing_ soccer, and he would like _being/to be_ a professional player.
4. We enjoy _gardening/to garden,_ so we _wouldn't/not_ like to live in an apartment.
5. I never go to classical concerts because I can't stand _listening/listen_ to classical music.
6. We'd like _to come/coming_ to your party next week, but we're really busy.
7. I usually cook because my husband _doesn't/wouldn't_ like doing it.
8. They're studying English because they'd like _getting/to get_ better jobs.
9. My girlfriend loves _going/go_ to the movies but she _doesn't/can't_ stand watching TV.

Vocabulary

8 Complete the sentences with words from Units 10–12. (The first letter of each word is given.)

Ex: You don't have to study this subject, it is o_ptional_____.

1. You have to take this class, it is c_____.
2. A k_____ is a class for very young children.
3. A p_____ is a university teacher.
4. You have to pay to study at a p_____ school.
5. A d_____ is a university certificate.
6. Breaking the traffic laws is an o_____.
7. After you pass the driving test you get a driver's l_____.
8. In many countries drivers have to wear a s_____ belt.
9. Africa isn't a country; it's a c_____.
10. Climbing a mountain is a c_____ experience.

9 Match the words to make phrases.

_____ 1. distance   a. climbing
_____ 2. mountain   b. learning
_____ 3. high   c. lights
_____ 4. swimming   d. pool
_____ 5. traffic   e. school

The Extra Listening Audio MP3 files and the Activity Worksheet are provided in the Student's *ActiveBook* disc and in the Teacher's *ActiveTeach* disc. The link for each unit is found on the Unit Wrap Up page. (A copy of the following Audioscript can also be found on those discs.) The Audio files are also provided at the end of the Audio Program CD.

UNIT 1

▶ 2.38

A: Look. Who is that?

B: Oh, that's Juan's sister. Her name is Mia.

A: Wow! She's really beautiful! How old is she?

B: I don't know. 20? 21? Let's find out. Hey Mia! Come here.

A: Be quiet!

B: Hi, Mia. This is my friend, Sam.

C: Hi, Sam! Nice to meet you.

B: Say something!

A: Um, uh, n-nice to meet you, Mia. Uh, where are you from?

C: I'm Colombian. And you?

A: I'm American and my daughter is, too.

B: You don't *have* a daughter!

A: Oh, I mean, my sister is, too. So, uh, Mia . . . what do you do?

C: I'm an artist. Right now I live with my aunt. She's married to an American.

A: Really? Cool!

UNIT 2

▶ 2.39

A: Welcome to Terrific Travel Agency. Can I help you?

B: What vacations do you have?

A: I have a great all-inclusive vacation at the Spring Club Resort Hotel. It's very nice. It's big and very modern.

B: What can you do there?

A: Well, let's see. OK, what time do you get up in the morning?

B: On vacation? I get up around ten-thirty or eleven.

A: OK, so you get up at eleven. Then you have breakfast in the fabulous restaurant.

B: Is the food good?

A: Yes, of course the food is good. Guests love it. Then you go outside and sit next to the pool. Do you like swimming?

B: Yes, I do. I love swimming.

A: Then swim and have lunch. You can eat by the pool.

B: What do you do in the evening?

A: After dinner, you can go to the nightclub. It's open until one-thirty.

B: It sounds great.

A: It is great! The hotel, your food, and all of your entertainment are included in one price.

B: Wow! How do I get there?

A: You go by plane. Of course the airplane cost is not included . . .

UNIT 3

▶ 2.40

A: Hey Sofia, wait. Hi. I'm Tom—from Min's party on Saturday?

B: Oh, yeah, Tom. Hi. How are you?

A: I'm fine, thanks. Listen are you busy next Thursday evening?

B: Yes, sorry. I'm a musician. I have to play in a concert Thursday evening at eight o'clock.

A: Really? A musician? That's great! What instrument do you play?

B: I play the cello. Do you play an instrument?

A: I play the guitar and I sing, but I'm not very good. Uh, what about the weekend? Are you free on Saturday?

B: I'm busy Saturday evening.

A: Oh, that's too bad.

B: Let me ask you a question. Can you dance?

A: Sure, I can dance. I love to dance.

B: OK then. Let's go dancing. Let's meet outside the club, Night Light, on Saturday evening at ten to ten.

A: Great. Where is it?

B: It's at 80 South Park Street.

A: Eighteen?

B: No, eighty. Let me give you my cell phone number. It's eight-two-eight, five-five-five, six-two-one-two.

A: OK. That's eight-two-eight, five-five-five, six-two-one-two. See you Saturday.

B: See you then. Bye.

UNIT 4

▶ 2.41

1. A: Hi, can I help you?
   B: Hello. I'd like a medium cheese pizza and a small salad.
   A: OK. Anything else?
   B: A bottle of water.

2. A: What can I get you?
   B: Do you have omelettes?
   A: Yes, we do.
   B: Can I have cheese in the omelette?
   A: Sure. Anything else?
   B: Some coffee.
   A: Small or large?
   B: Large, please.

3. A: Mommy, I want some ice cream!
   B: No, I'd like you to eat an apple.
   A: No! I want pizza!
   B: How about a glass of milk?
   A: I want chocolate milk and chocolate chip cookies and . . .

4. A: I'd like three pounds of ground beef, a pound of chicken, two fish . . .
   B: We don't have any fish today.
   A: OK. Then I need a quarter pound of cheese, four sticks of butter, and two loaves of bread . . .

UNIT 5

▶ **2.42**

A: I live north of the city in the mountains. I love the mountains. It's not noisy—it's quiet. It's really beautiful. I can relax and have fun here.

I have an unusual house. Why is it unusual? My house is very, very small. The house is only 140 square feet. There's one bedroom upstairs. Downstairs there is a living room, a dining room, and a kitchen—all in one room. You can cook in the kitchen. You can even take a shower in the kitchen. There's a sink, a small fridge, a microwave, a small washing machine and one cabinet. I have a small CD player. There are two small armchairs next to a table. I have a closet and a desk. I have a small front porch. I like to eat and relax there. There's no garage. There isn't a yard, but there is a forest—a really big forest. I love my house. It's small but it's very comfortable and quiet.

UNIT 6

▶ 2.43

1. A: Excuse me.

   B: Yes, can I help you?

   A: Where are the children's shoes?

   B: Children's shoes are on the fourth floor. Go straight and you'll see the escalator on your left. Take it to the fourth floor. Children's shoes are on the right.

   A: Thanks.

2. A: Excuse me, is there a newsstand near here?

   B: There was a newsstand across the street, but last month they moved it. Now it's on the next street. Go straight one block. Turn left at the light. It's half a block down on your right.

   A: Thanks.

3. A: Your room is so messy!

   B: Mom! Don't!

   A: Just look at this room! There are dirty socks on your desk; there are dirty dishes on your bed. There's a cup of cold coffee and some chocolates on your chair. Clean this room!

   B: Mom, I started but I didn't finish. I decided to finish my work. I had a lot of homework.

   A: Well, finish it right now or no computer for you tonight.

   B: OK.

4. A: Alicia, where were you? Were you at the library?

   B: No, I wasn't. I was at Linda's house. Linda's new house. She moved last weekend.

   A: You didn't tell us that she moved.

   B: Sorry, Dad. I forgot.

UNIT 7

▶ 2.44

Exercise 1

1. I think the CDs are next to the sink.
2. Amelia is not in class. She's sick.
3. Buy three books and get the fourth one free!
4. I'd like some food but first, a bottle of water, please. I have a terrible thirst.
5. When I was young, we had three beautiful trees in our yard.

Exercise 2

1. They're not Amanda's books. The books are theirs.
2. A: Does this book belong to you?
   B: Yes, it's my.
3. Are these keys mine or your?
4. A: Does this umbrella belong to you?
   B: Excuse me?
   A: Is it yours?

Exercise 3

1. this
2. that
3. think
4. with
5. teeth
6. cloth
7. these
8. those
9. tenth

UNIT 8

▶ 2.45

A: Hello?

B: Hi Marta, It's Jacob. What are you doing?

A: I'm out walking. What are you doing?

B: I'm preparing dinner and watching TV.

A: Uh-oh, the sun isn't shining now. The weather is starting to look cloudy.

B: Hold on, I'm checking the weather report.

A: I'm listening.

B: Wow, walk fast. Or maybe run.

A: Oh, no! Why?

B: The weather is changing. It's getting colder and it's snowing pretty near to you on the map. What are you wearing?

A: I usually wear sneakers, jeans and a shirt, a wool sweater and a hat when I walk. You know—layers. I hardly ever wear shorts. But today I put on shorts and a cotton T-shirt. The sun was shining, and it was hot this morning. Now, it's cloudy and it isn't warm and . . . Oh, no, it's snowing!

B: Really? Wow! Run! Call me when you get home.

A: OK. Bye!

UNIT 9

▶ 2.46

A: Excuse me? Hi.

B: Yes?

A: I'm here doing a survey about movies. Can I ask you some questions?

B: Sure.

A: Thanks. Ok, well, what is one of your favorite movies?

B: I guess I would say *Avatar*. I like *Avatar* better than any other movie I've seen for awhile.

A: Have you seen many movies this year?

B: Yeah, I think I've seen about eight or nine movies. *Avatar* is still the best one.

A: What kind of movies do you like? You know, do you prefer action movies or comedies?

B: Oh, I prefer action movies. And thrillers, too. I think that *The Dark Knight* was the scariest movie I've seen in a long time. Who's the craziest, scariest villain I've seen in a movie? The Joker in *The Dark Knight*.

A: Yeah, he was pretty scary. Which do you like better, going out to the movies or staying home and watching TV?

B: I like staying at home better than going to the movies. It's more convenient and it's cheaper. Movie theaters are noisier. But going to the movies is more exciting than staying home. So if I have money I'll go out. If I don't, I'll stay home.

A: Thanks so much for talking with us.

B: No problem.

UNIT 10

▶ 2.47

A: This is my first real vacation in three years! I'm so excited! Where can we go?

B: Well . . . let's see. Where have you been?

A: I've been hiking in the mountains. My sister and I went last summer for two days.

B: I think hiking's a little boring. Let's do something exciting. Have you ever been bungee jumping?

A: No, I haven't, and I never will. I like my legs and don't want to lose them doing something dangerous, thanks.

B: OK. No bungee jumping. I know! How about going to Mexico? I think Oaxaca is the most beautiful city in the world, and it won't be crowded right now. Have you ever seen bull riding?

A: No, I haven't. Is it scary?

B: Actually, it's very exciting, but it's pretty sad, too.

A: I don't think I want to see bull riding, but I like trying restaurants and the food is good, right?

B: It's amazing! Oaxaca has some of the best food in the country.

A: What's the price for a ticket to Oaxaca?

B: You know, the tickets aren't too expensive. Round trip air fare is about six hundred and fifty dollars.

A: Hmm. Is it a really long flight?

B: No, it isn't. About five hours. They have some first class resorts. They're really luxurious. . .

A: Are they far from the airport? Waiting for a bus is boring but taking a taxi is expensive.

B: We'll see. For sightseeing in the city, the cheapest way to travel is going on foot.

A: OK, then. Sounds great. Let's go.

B: Yay! Oaxaca, here we come!

UNIT 11

▶ 2.48

A: The rules of the road are different from country to country. In some countries it's very easy to get a driver's license. In others, like Brazil, it's pretty difficult. What do you have to do to get a driver's license in Brazil? Here are some of the rules: First you have to be 18 years old or more. Then you will have to take the driving test. But in Brazil, there are four different steps to this test. The first step is a medical test to show you are healthy enough to drive. They test your eyes and so forth. The second step is a mental test to show how you think and to make sure you can solve problems. The third step is a course about traffic rules and driving theory. When you have finished about 45 hours of theory course, you take a written test. Then you are ready for the fourth and last step. The last step is taking actual driving lessons. After many hours of driving practice, you take a driving test. If you pass all of these different steps then you can finally get a Brazilian driver's license.

UNIT 12

▶ 2.49

A: What are you reading?

B: A book about the rainforest. When I graduate from college in June, I want to travel to Brazil and see the rainforest.

A: What are you going to do there?

B: I'm going to go hiking and photograph nature. I'm also going to learn Portuguese. I want to study Portuguese, Spanish, and Italian and write my first book before I'm thirty.

A: Wow! How long are you going to be there?

B: For about a month. And when I've traveled all over Brazil, I'll go to Argentina. Why don't you come with me? We can study and travel together.

A: Really? I'd love to go traveling. I enjoy hiking. I'd like to see the endangered animals in the rainforest. I'm very interested in Golden Lion Tamarins. They're the very small monkeys with red fur and golden faces.

A: I love those monkeys.

B: Me, too. They're so cute.